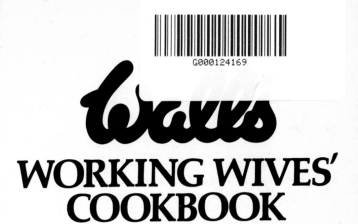

WORKING WIVES' COOKBOOK

JANET WARREN

A Martin Book

Published by Martin Books
8 Market Passage, Cambridge CB2 3PF
in association with
The Wall's Meat Company Ltd
Malthouse Walk, Banbury, Oxon OX16 8QL

First published 1981
© The Wall's Meat Company Ltd and Janet Warren 1981
ISBN 0 85941 157 5

The author would like to thank the following for their help in the
compilation of this book: The Microwave Oven Association;
TI Creda Ltd; Anchor Hocking; and the organisations who kindly
supplied photographs.

Cover picture and photographs on pp. 7, 19, 23, 31, 59, 63, 67, 75,
79, 87, 91 and 95 by John Lee; p. 27 from Danish Agricultural
Producers; pp. 39, 43 and 47 from the British Sausage Bureau;
p. 51 from the British Bacon Bureau; p. 71 from the Pasta
Information Centre.

Illustrations by Tom Bailey
Design by Ken Vail Graphic Design
Typesetting by Rowland Phototypesetting Ltd, Bury St Edmunds
Printed and bound in Great Britain by
Morrison & Gibb Limited, Edinburgh

CONTENTS

AUTHOR'S NOTE

Please remember the following points when using any of the recipes in this book.

1 *Spoon measures* All measurements of teaspoons, dessert-spoons and tablespoons are level unless otherwise stated.

2 *Metrication* The list of ingredients in every recipe is in dual marking, i.e. imperial (oz, fl oz, etc) and metric (g, ml, etc). Please use one set or the other in any one recipe; never mix the two and never compare the conversion from one recipe to another as sometimes they can differ. The metric weights and measures are in rounded amounts for easy use, except in the case of products sold in exact metric quantities, where the weight actually on the pack is given.

3 *Symbols* To help you quickly select a recipe which fits in with the amount of time you have at your disposal, the time taken to prepare and cook the dish has been featured at the beginning of each recipe, with symbols to make them easy to pick out:

 PREPARATION TIME

 COOKING TIME(S)

Where it is possible to use labour-saving devices to make the preparation or cooking easier or quicker, a note of these appears also at the beginning of the recipe, preceded by a third symbol:

🐃 LABOUR-SAVING EQUIPMENT

Introduction

Every working wife in the land is faced, at some time or other, with the major problem of giving the family something to eat which requires the minimum of time spent shopping, preparing and cooking but which can always be relied upon to produce a successful result. Wall's, as leading manufacturers of fresh and frozen meat-based products, are very aware of this problem. Much of the success of any finished dish, not only in its appearance and taste but also in its nutritional content, is determined by the quality of the basic ingredients. As you will see from this book, Wall's vast range of products is ideal for the busy wife. The products are very adaptable, easy to cook and, best of all, readily available throughout the country.

Being a working wife myself, with a house and family to look after, I, too, am aware of all the pitfalls and problems one can be faced with. My aim, in the next few chapters, is to guide you in the right direction, and to make life easier for you, with lots of hints and useful recipes. At the beginning of each recipe I have highlighted the preparation and cooking times so that you can see at a glance the time involved in making the dish for the family. I have also made as much use as possible of the various labour-saving pieces of equipment now available. These are explained in greater detail on pp. 12–14.

The keynote for any working wife who successfully combines a job with the running of a home is organisation. The paragraphs that follow describe in detail the areas where I think being organised is all-important.

THE HOUSEWORK

The saying 'a problem shared is a problem halved' applies very well to housework. If the family can share the tasks involved in the running of the home then the working wife can spend a little more time enjoying life with the family. Here are a few areas that I consider can be shared.

1 Children should be encouraged to make their own beds and keep their rooms tidy.
2 Perhaps your husband or even one of the older children could occasionally cook the meal so that you can have an evening off.
3 Even the younger children can help when it comes to laying the table and the teenagers should be able to tackle the job of preparing the vegetables.
4 The task of washing up can be shared.
5 Other members of the family can sometimes do the shopping.
6 Teach the children to keep their own shoes clean.

SHOPPING

Shopping can be a major problem for any working wife, as often the only times available are the lunch hour, late night opening or at the weekends. All of these are the busiest times in the stores and, therefore, can result in a very lengthy operation. A few tips to cut the time down are:

1 Get to know your shops so that you don't waste time locating the various items.
2 Although you may save a little money shopping around, you certainly won't save time and often, for us working wives, time is money.
3 If you have enough storage space and, obviously, a car to carry the purchases home, try to cut down your main shopping to once a month, leaving only the perishable items to the weekly or daily shop.
4 Always plan your menus and check your kitchen stock before you go to the shops and do try to keep to the list. It will make catering easier in the long run.
5 When writing your shopping list, try and group together items that are stacked near to each other in the store so that you don't have to retrace your steps too often.

A selection of pre-packed meat products and convenience foods which are invaluable to the working wife's store cupboard. A delicious and nourishing meal can quickly be prepared by combining one of them with fresh vegetables

6 Always keep a jotter pad close at hand in your kitchen. As you use a can or packet of food, or get low in items such as flour and sugar, you can make a note immediately for the next shopping trip, and thus avoid running short of anything.

Weekly Shopping Checklist

Although the items on anyone's shopping list reflect the family's personal tastes, below are listed a few of the items a working wife would probably use constantly and therefore have to replace. Use this guide for checking when writing your own shopping list, in conjunction with those in the store cupboard, fridge and freezer sections which follow.

Cereals	Cooking oil	Cakes
Marmalade and jams	Vinegar	Bread
Flour	Chutney and pickles	Fresh vegetables
Cornflour	Mustard	Fresh meat
Sugar	Herbs and spices	Fruit cordials
Coffee	Salt and pepper	Cleaning materials
Tea	Biscuits	

THE STORE CUPBOARD

A well stocked store cupboard is invaluable to the working wife as she will often have to produce 'instant' meals, but that doesn't mean the continual use of only convenience foods. Many delicious dishes can be created using a packet or can in conjunction with fresh foods. Here are just a few samples – one for each day of the week.

1 *Summer Soup.* Chill a can of tomato soup well and flavour just before serving with grated orange rind and juice.

2 *Seashore Pâté.* With a fork, mix a can of pilchards in tomato sauce with lemon juice, and a little Worcestershire sauce if liked. Serve with freshly made toast.

3 *Shepherd's Pie.* Mix together a can of minced beef with dried onion flakes and top with instant mashed potatoes flavoured with grated cheese. Bake at 375°F/190°C/Gas Mark 5 for 20–30 minutes.

4 *Sweet or Savoury Crumble.* Use a pastry mix dry-blended with chopped nuts and sprinkle this over a can of fruit pie filling; or serve the pastry mix blended with cheese or herbs as a savoury crumble.

5 *Bean Salad.* Mix a can of drained butter beans with flaked tuna fish, onion rings, black olives and Thousand Island dressing.

6 *Apricot Nectar*. Warm canned apricots with cream and brandy; sprinkle with browned flaked almonds before serving.

7 *Sponge Pudding Special*. Heat together butter, sugar and golden syrup until well blended. Add slices of canned sponge pudding; cook them, turning frequently, until golden brown and caramelised.

Store Cupboard Checklist

Always remember to keep a constant check on the items in the store cupboard. It is a good idea to date each new purchase so that cans and packets can be used in rotation and none get overlooked. Below is a general guide to the storage life of canned and packet items, which can also be used as a shopping checklist.

Canned meat pie filling	2 years
Corned beef, ham and other canned solid meat	up to 5 years
Meat and vegetable meals	2 years
Canned fish in oil	up to 5 years
Canned fish in tomato sauce	up to 1 year
Canned pasta in sauce	2 years
Canned vegetables	2 years
Canned fruit, most kinds	1–2 years
Canned rhubarb	9 months
Canned milk puddings	12 months
Canned sponge puddings	2 years
Dried peas, beans and lentils	6–12 months
Instant mashed potato	6 months
Canned soup	2 years
Packet soup	12 months
Dried milk	9–12 months
Evaporated milk	12 months
Instant desserts	12 months
Jellies	9–12 months
Cake mixes	9 months
Pastry mixes	6 months

THE REFRIGERATOR

I think the refrigerator is the most essential and useful of all the pieces of equipment a working wife can have in the kitchen. It can extend the life of perishable foods by keeping them cool, clean and away from insects. It eliminates wastage, since surplus food can be saved and used either as the basis of another meal or cold the next day. It enables you to store many partially or completely prepared dishes until required. Last, but not least, as the refrigerator maintains a temperature below 10°C bacterial activity is limited and the life of the vitamins and minerals in food is extended.

However, as with all the equipment in the kitchen, there are a few basic rules which must be followed:

1 Never put hot food into the refrigerator, because this will give off steam which quickly freezes, causing rapid icing.

2 Always cover the food you put in the refrigerator: the low temperature tends to draw out the moisture, drying the food surface quicker than normal and also causing excessive ice build-up on the evaporator.

3 Avoid storing strong-smelling foods, such as pineapple, strawberries or onions, in the refrigerator. However well they are wrapped, the flavour can be transferred.

4 Try to use the various temperature zones in the refrigerator to store food items in the most suitable place. Raw meat, fish and offal should go in the coldest part just below the evaporator; cooking fats, cooked foods and cheese are best stored in the main section; milk, eggs, butter and drinks go in their special racks; and, lastly, salads, vegetables and fruit need the vegetable drawer or hydrator.

Refrigerator Stocking Checklist

Eggs	Cooking fats	Wall's sausages
Milk	Cream	Wall's cold sliced meats
Cheese	Margarine	Yogurts
Butter	Wall's bacon	Salad ingredients

Recommended Refrigerator Storage Times

Use these dates as an approximate guide to the lifespan of the various items listed below. Many packaged dairy goods are date stamped, so do look out for the manufacturers' recommended dates.

Eggs	up to 6 weeks
Milk	4–5 days
Cheese – hard	up to 1 week
– soft	2–3 days
Butter – unsalted	2 weeks
– salted	3 weeks
Cooking fats	6 months
Cream, unopened	3–4 days
Margarine	up to 2 months

Wall's bacon, once opened	3 days
Wall's sausages	3 days
Wall's cold meats, once opened	3 days
Yogurts	1 week
Salad ingredients	
tomatoes	1 week
unwashed lettuce	2–3 days
cucumber	3–5 days
watercress	1 day

THE FREEZER

A freezer is such a boon for anyone who leads a very busy life, as it can be used in so many ways to save time.

1 Recipes can be made in double quantity, so that one meal can be frozen for another time.

2 Cakes, bakes and bread store very well and are handy to have available when time is short. Keep a sliced loaf in the freezer as it can be used from frozen to make toast.

3 If the family takes sandwiches for packed lunches, make a month's supply at a time to save that daily, time-consuming chore – but avoid any of the wet fillings such as tomatoes, cucumber, etc. If you put the frozen sandwiches in a lunch box in the morning, they will be thawed out and perfect to eat by lunchtime.

4 Look out for specially prepared freezer packs: they can save considerable money and shopping time. Wall's sell large packs of sausages, all of which are individually frozen for easy use, which allows them to be cooked straight from the freezer. Just grill or fry slowly as instructed until golden brown, making sure, of course, that they are cooked through.

5 The packs of Wall's pastry topped and potato topped pies, pasties, sausage rolls and flans are very useful for the working wife, because they also can be taken straight from the freezer to the oven to cook.

6 Always label and date every item in the freezer so that, at a glance, you know what it is and how long you have had it.

Freezer Checklist

Meat	Wall's pies, pasties, flans	Cakes and bakes
Vegetables		Uncooked pastry
Fruit	Wall's sausage rolls	Beefburgers
Wall's sausages	Double cream	Fish fingers
Wall's bacon joints, rashers	Wall's ice cream	
	Bread, rolls	

Guide to Storage Life of Frozen Foods

Meats	
Beef and lamb (uncooked)	12 months
Pork (uncooked)	9 months
Chicken (uncooked)	12 months
Mince and offal (uncooked)	2 months
Wall's sausages	3 months
Wall's bacon joints	3 months
Wall's bacon rashers, steaks	3 months
Prepared meat dishes	2 months

Fish	
White fish (cod, haddock, etc.)	6–12 months
Oily fish (mackerel, trout, etc.)	4 months

Vegetables	
Home or commercially frozen	12 months

Fruit	
Poached in syrup or dry sugar	12 months

Dairy produce	
Eggs (not in the shell)	6 months
Butter (unsalted)	6 months
(salted)	3 months
Double cream	3–4 months
Soft cheese	8 months
Hard cheese	3 months

Prepared foods	
Soups	4 months
Cakes and coded pastry	6 months
Uncooked pastry	3 months
Bread (sliced)	3 months
(French)	1 month
Ice cream	3 months

LABOUR-SAVING EQUIPMENT

There are many pieces of labour-saving equipment available nowadays and it is the working wife who should take full advantage of them. Throughout the book I have given, in addition to the conventional method of cooking, ways of using any of the following appliances which may be suitable.

Automatic Cooker

This can be a very useful piece of equipment for the working wife. Instead of having to serve meals quickly cooked after she comes back from work, she can prepare in advance a casserole or pie, or even put in a piece of meat to roast, before going out. The oven switches itself on automatically while she is still out and the family can come home to delicious smells wafting their way around the kitchen. Remember, however, to:

(a) allow an extra 15 minutes to the normal cooking time to allow the oven to heat up;

(b) set the oven temperature as well as the auto timer.

Mixer/Liquidiser

Undoubtedly a great time saver as it can be getting on with one job while you are doing something else. Both the mixer and liquidiser also save a lot of physical effort, which, if you've come home from work tired, is very welcome.

Infra-red Grill

Very quick and easy to use, infra-red grills are ideal when it comes to cooking a meal speedily. They can grill bacon, burgers and bacon steaks in minutes and also are excellent to use when toasting sandwiches. If you are thinking of purchasing one, make sure the plates are Teflon-coated and can be easily removed for washing up.

Microwave Oven

This is a relatively new piece of equipment in its domestic form, but one many working wives should find useful, especially in conjunction with a freezer – frozen food can be thawed in minutes rather than hours. It cannot replace the conventional cooker, but should be used alongside it. It requires a totally different way of cooking. It is superb when it comes to reheating dishes – ideal if the family tend to come in at different times for their meals – and so safe that even the children can use it. As microwave ovens do vary slightly from make to make, ensure you have completely mastered the use of your particular model before you start.

Pressure Cookers

These labour-saving devices have been on the market for many years and with time they have developed enormously, to include safety valves and now even auto timers. The majority of British-made models work on the three-weight system (5 lb, 10 lb and 15 lb), but the Continental pressure cookers, although working on the same system, only reach 7½ lb pressure, which means that their cooking times are longer for some recipes. Do check in your instruction book before starting.

Slow Cookers

Not only do slow cookers cook food beautifully but they also use only as much energy as a light bulb, so that you save on electricity as well. There are many varieties available in different sizes and if you don't mind preparing the evening meal at the same time as serving the breakfast you will find a slow cooker very useful. Another big advantage of slow cookers is that the food never seems to spoil and so if, again, you have to feed the family at varying times, a casserole simmering away in a slow cooker is ideal. Incidentally, if you are thinking of purchasing a slow cooker, I would suggest you go for one with a removable casserole dish, which will look more attractive when taken to the table.

NUTRITION

A well balanced diet is essential for anyone who wants to lead a busy, active life and, although you don't have to know the finer details of the nutrient content of every food, it is very useful to have at least some idea.

We all need to eat food to provide energy and ensure that our bodies function properly. The nutrients needed to carry out these tasks are found in all sorts of food and as long as we keep to a varied diet, the rest will look after itself.

The energy we need is often measured in Calories and the amount of energy each person requires is affected by their age, sex, height, weight and work. Below is a rough guide to what different people need daily.

Age	Males	Females
3 years old	1,600 Calories	1,600 Calories
15 years old	3,000 Calories	2,300 Calories
20–60 years old (active life)	3,600 Calories	2,500 Calories
20–60 years old (sedentary life)	2,700 Calories	2,100 Calories

Basically, there are three groups of nutrients that provide energy – proteins, fats and carbohydrates. There are also numerous vitamins and minerals, necessary only in small amounts, that are essential for the development and maintenance of a healthy body. Below are listed some of the fresh foods in which these nutrients can be found. Do also read the sides of packets of convenience foods – increasingly these are giving a guide to the nutrient content of the food.

Nutrient	Functions	Sources
Proteins	Provide material for growth, tissue repair and bone development; also provide energy	Meat, fish, cheese, eggs, peas, beans, nuts
Fats	Provide energy and help cell growth	Butter, oil, margarine, milk, cheese, bacon, ham, fish, meats
Carbohydrates	Provide energy	Bread, biscuits, cereals, cakes, rice, pasta, potatoes, sugar
Vitamin A	Important for healthy eyes, lungs, etc.; aids growth	Fish liver oil, animal liver and kidney, spinach, dairy produce, eggs, watercress, carrots
B Vitamins	Important for general health and vitality. Helps body to convert food into energy	Milk, cheese, eggs, bread, yeast, meat (especially liver and kidney)
Vitamin C	Maintains healthy tissue	Oranges, lemons, blackcurrant and raw or partially cooked green vegetables
Vitamin D	Aids bone development	Margarine, oily fish, eggs, butter, liver
Iron	Aids the use of oxygen in the bloodstream	Liver, meat, bread, eggs, green vegetables, potatoes
Calcium	Important for healthy teeth, bones and muscles	Milk, cheese, flour, bread, green vegetables

Breakfasts and Brunches

THE WEEKDAY BREAKFAST

The variety of foods that can be quickly cooked and served for breakfast is enormous. Start the meal with fruit juice, grapefruit or a cereal, if time permits, and then choose any combination of the items listed below, depending on the size of breakfast you and the family want. I have included an easy-to-use chart which sums up the cooking and preparation methods and times for these essential breakfast ingredients. Eggs, which can be served in a number of different ways, are dealt with separately below.

Bacon

Basically, three cuts of bacon rashers are available in two different cures and the one you select depends on your family's tastes. Streaky bacon rashers contain almost the same amount of lean meat as fat, and it is the fat content that actually provides most of the flavour. For a leaner rasher select Prime Back, Back or Half Gammon. A combination pack is also available, called Wall's Middle Bacon, which gives you rashers of both back and streaky. Wall's offer both British and Danish Bacon, easily recognised by their respective blue and red packs. The British cure is mild and sweet, and the Danish bacon is very consistent in quality, flavour and leanness.

Sausages
The choice of sausages on the market is vast and, as with bacon, it depends on your family's tastes and needs. Wall's produce the traditional thick sausages (eight to the pound) in Pork, Pork and Beef, Pork and Turkey, Pork with Herbs recipes. An alternative is the family pack, with ten sausages to the pound. Then there are the smaller sausages (sixteen to the pound) – chipolatas (in the South) or links (in the North). The other packs which are very popular, especially with the children, are the skinless varieties, available in Pork or Pork and Beef.

Black Pudding
This is sold in rings ready-sliced, in tray packs or in small 6 oz packets and is delicious served for breakfast.

Mushrooms
Allow 1–2 oz/25–50 g mushrooms per person, depending on the amount of the other constituents of the breakfast. I prefer to serve the flat mushrooms for breakfast, as they have more flavour.

Tomatoes
Serve fried or grilled as an accompaniment to other cooked breakfast foods. Alternatively, as a change, slice and serve on toast, or fresh buttered wholemeal bread, sprinkled with seasoning and a little chopped parsley.

Eggs
Eggs form the basis of a variety of breakfasts that are all very easy and quick to cook.
Boiled Place the eggs (preferably at room temperature) into simmering water with a little salt. Cook for 3–5 minutes after the water boils, depending on the degree of hardness the family likes.
Fried Heat a little lard in a frying pan or, better still, use the fat left in the pan from frying the bacon. Break in the egg, reduce the heat and cook until set, basting occasionally with fat so that it cooks evenly.
Poached Heat a pan at least half full of water and, when it comes to the boil, add a few drops of vinegar. Then, stir the water with a spoon, until it spins. Add the eggs, one at a time, in to the centre of the pan so that the motion of the water keeps the white around the egg yolk. Cook for 2–3 minutes until set.

Remove on a draining spoon and serve on buttered toast or perhaps with sliced ham or a poached haddock.

Scrambled   The most essential piece of equipment when cooking scrambled egg is a non-stick pan – it makes washing up so easy. If you are making scrambled egg for several people who arrive at the breakfast table at different times, make the full amount required in one go then stir a little single cream through the portions left so that they can be kept warm, without curdling, until required.

Here are two recipes for scrambled eggs, using conventional methods and using a microwave oven. Allow 1–2 eggs per person.

Ordinary method:
½ oz/15 g butter
2 eggs (size 2)
2 tablespoons/2 × 15 ml spoon milk
salt and pepper

Heat the butter in the pan, add the milk, then break in the eggs and beat them well with a plastic spoon or spatula. Add seasoning, return the pan to the heat and, stirring all the time, cook the mixture until creamy and almost set. Serve on hot, buttered toast.

Microwave method:
Using the same ingredients as for the ordinary method, beat the eggs and milk together in a bowl, add the butter and seasoning, then cover the bowl with cling film and cook the eggs for 2–3 minutes, stirring them once.

French Toast or Eggy Bread   Allow 1–2 slices per person.

1 egg (size 2)
1 tablespoon/15 ml spoon milk
salt and pepper
2 slices white or brown bread, crusts removed
1 oz/25 g butter

Beat the egg and milk together with plenty of seasoning. Pour the liquid on to a plate, then dip the slices of bread into it one at a time so they are completely coated. Heat the butter in a frying pan, add the egg soaked slices and fry them for a few minutes on each side until golden brown and crispy. Delicious served with bacon or tomatoes.

A satisfying British breakfast

Breakfast Preparation Chart

Food	Preparation	Preparation time	Frying	Grilling	Microwave oven	Automatic cooker
Bacon	Cut rind off streaky rashers.	30 secs	Place rashers in pan with lean meat of 1 rasher covering fat of next. Fry 3 mins, turning often.	Place rasher on rack with fat covering lean; grill 4 mins.	Put rasher on plate and cover with paper towel; cook 1 min per rasher.	–
Sausages	Separate but do not prick skins. Place sausages in cold fat, in cold pan, when frying.	30 secs	Cook over a medium heat and turn frequently. Thicks 15–20 mins, chipolatas or links and skinless 10–15 mins.	Cook under a preheated grill, turning frequently; times as for frying.	–	Put sausages in small baking tin and set at 350°F/ 180°C/Gas Mark 4 for 30–45 mins.
Black pudding	Cut into ¼ in./ 5 cm slices.	1 min.	Fry in bacon fat for a few mins on each side.	Grill on an oiled rack and brush with more oil during cooking; 2 mins each side.	–	–

Food	Preparation	Preparation time	Frying	Grilling	Microwave oven	Automatic cooker
Mushrooms	Wipe with damp cloth; do not peel but trim stalk; then slice, quarter or leave whole.	3 mins	Fry sliced, quartered or whole in a little fat; 1–5 mins.	Use only whole mushrooms; place on oiled rack, dot with butter, season and cook 3–5 mins.	Place 4 oz/100 g in cook-bag with ½ oz/15 g butter; cook 1 min.	–
Tomatoes	Cut in half.	1 min.	Place cut side down in pan with melted fat; brown quickly, turn over and complete cooking – 2 mins. Sprinkle with salt before serving.	As for frying.	–	–

THE WEEKEND BREAKFAST – BRUNCH

With the arrival of the weekend, 'brunch' is the ideal meal to serve in the morning, halfway between what would normally be breakfast and lunch. It is the perfect excuse to have a marvellous fry-up of bacon, sausages, eggs and so on, or perhaps to try something a little more adventurous from the recipes which follow.

Begin the meal with grapefruit cocktail, porridge, or home-made muesli accompanied by milk, yogurt and fresh fruit. Then serve the main course and complete the brunch with fresh toast and rolls, or perhaps croissants, not forgetting the tea or coffee (or, as a change, hot chocolate topped with whipped cream and ground cinnamon).

Home-made Muesli
Serves 10

 PREPARATION TIME: 5 minutes

I always make a fairly large quantity of muesli at one time, as it keeps so well in an airtight container. This particular recipe is the one that is most popular in my household. Your family may prefer it sweeter or perhaps less crunchy – it really doesn't matter, just use these quantities as a basic guide and experiment until you find what you all consider to be the right mix.

8 oz/225 g rolled porridge oats
2 oz/50 g wheatgerm
2 oz/50 g cleaned sultanas
1 oz/25 g block dates, chopped
4 oz/100 g toasted oat cereal
1 oz/25 g walnuts chopped
1 oz/25 g wheat bran
1 tablespoon/15 ml spoon skimmed milk powder

Put all the ingredients in the airtight container to be used, put on the lid and shake them about until thoroughly mixed. Store in a dry place until required and then turn into a large serving bowl. Serve with fresh milk, natural yogurt and fresh fruit.

Brunch dishes: Home-made Muesli, Bacon and Haddock Kedgeree, Potato Cakes and Tasty Scrambled Egg, served with sausages and grilled tomatoes

Bacon and Haddock Kedgeree
Serves 4

○ PREPARATION TIME: 10 minutes

● COOKING TIME: 10 minutes

☛ LABOUR-SAVING EQUIPMENT: Microwave oven

7.05 oz/200 g packet Wall's Streaky Bacon Rashers
2 oz/50 g butter
4 oz/100 g long-grain rice, cooked
2 eggs, hard-boiled
8 oz/225 g smoked cod or haddock, poached
1 tablespoon/15 ml spoon fresh chopped parsley
freshly ground black pepper
lemon wedges

Cut the rind from the bacon rashers and fry them over a medium heat until brown. Keeping four rashers on one side, chop the rest into 1 in./2.5 cm pieces and return them to the pan.

Add the butter and when it has melted stir in the rice. Shell and chop the eggs, flake the poached fish (removing any skin or bones) and then stir both these ingredients into the pan, together with the parsley and black pepper. Stirring all the time, heat the ingredients thoroughly. Turn them into a warm serving dish and garnish with the reserved bacon rashers and the lemon wedges before serving.

Microwave Place the bacon in a shallow glass dish, cover with a piece of kitchen paper and cook for 5 minutes. Remove four rashers to use for decoration, and chop the rest and return them to the bowl with the butter. Cover and cook for a minute to melt, stir in the other ingredients and cook for 5 minutes, turning them occasionally so that they heat evenly.

Tasty Scrambled Egg
Serves 4

 PREPARATION TIME: 3 minutes

 COOKING TIME: 5 minutes

☛ LABOUR-SAVING EQUIPMENT: Microwave oven

6 eggs (size 2)
4 fl oz/120 ml single cream
salt and cayenne pepper
1 teaspoon/5 ml spoon made English mustard
1 teaspoon/5 ml spoon Worcestershire sauce
1 oz/25 g butter

Beat the eggs and then mix in the cream, salt, cayenne pepper, mustard and Worcestershire sauce. Melt the butter, add the egg mixture and cook over a low heat, stirring almost all the time until scrambled. Serve with fried black pudding.
Microwave The real advantage of using a microwave for scrambled eggs is that there is only the bowl to wash up afterwards and not a nasty saucepan. Put all the ingredients into a bowl and beat them thoroughly together. Cook the scrambled egg for 5 minutes, stirring it once or twice for an even mix.

Potato Cakes
Serves 4 (makes 10 cakes, 3 for each adult and 2 for each child)

PREPARATION TIME: 5 minutes

COOKING TIME: 20 minutes

1 lb/450 g parboiled potatoes, peeled
4 oz/113 g packet Wall's Chopped Pork and Ham
2 eggs, size 2
salt and pepper
a pinch of nutmeg
1 oz/25 g butter
2 tablespoons/2 × 15 ml spoon oil

Coarsely grate the potato into a bowl. Chop the sliced meat, mix it into the potato and then bind the two ingredients together with the eggs. Season the mixture well, adding the nutmeg.

Heat the butter and oil together in a pan and place spoonfuls of the mixture into the hot fat. Cook each cake for about 5 minutes on each side, to brown nicely. Keep the first batch warm while cooking the rest, and then serve them all with fried eggs.

Copenhagen Platter
Serves 4

 PREPARATION TIME: 10 minutes

 COOKING TIME: 10 minutes

7.05 oz/200 g packet Wall's Middle Cut Danish Bacon Rashers
2 oz/50 g butter
1 oz/25 g plain flour
¼ pint/150 ml milk
11 oz/325 g packet chopped frozen spinach, thawed
salt and freshly ground black pepper
8 oz/225 g button mushrooms, washed and trimmed
6 eggs scrambled (see p. 18)
1 tomato, sliced
a few chopped chives (optional)

Cut the rind and any small bones from the bacon rashers and then grill them until golden brown.

Meanwhile, melt half the butter in a pan, blend in the flour and, off the heat, gradually stir in the milk to make a smooth consistency. Over the heat, and stirring all the time, bring the sauce to the boil; then add the spinach with plenty of seasoning and simmer for a few minutes until thoroughly heated. Cook the mushrooms in the remaining butter, until tender.

To serve, arrange the spinach, scrambled eggs, bacon rashers and mushrooms in a warm dish and garnish with the sliced tomato and the chives, if available.

Copenhagen Platter

Sausage and Kidney Turbigo
Serves 4

○ PREPARATION TIME: 20 minutes

● COOKING TIMES:
Normal: 20 minutes
Pressure cooker: 5 minutes

☛ LABOUR-SAVING EQUIPMENT: Pressure cooker

4 lamb's kidneys
2 tablespoons/2 × 15 ml spoon oil
1 oz/25 g margarine
4 oz/100 g Wall's Streaky Bacon Rashers
8 oz/227 g packet Wall's Pork Chipolatas
1 large onion, peeled and chopped
4 oz/100 g button mushrooms, washed and trimmed
1 tablespoon/15 ml spoon plain flour
1 tablespoon/15 ml spoon tomato ketchup
½ pint/300 ml stock
1 bay leaf
salt and pepper

Remove the skin and core from the kidneys, halve them and cut each half into two. Heat the oil and margarine, fry the kidneys until sealed and transfer to a plate.

Cut the rind and any small bones from the bacon rashers and cut each into four; fry the pieces with the chipolatas until both are brown. Transfer to the plate with the kidneys.

Fry the onions and mushrooms in the remaining fat and when they start to brown stir in the flour; then, off the heat, mix in the tomato ketchup and gradually blend in the stock. Return the pan to the heat and, stirring all the time, bring the sauce to the boil. Add the bay leaf and check for seasoning.

Return the kidneys, bacon and chipolatas to the pan, cover it and simmer the turbigo for 20–25 minutes until all the ingredients are tender. Garnish the dish with toast triangles and chopped parsley before serving.

Pressure cooker Brown all the ingredients as in the normal method, but using the pressure cooker, and transfer the onions and mushrooms to the plate with the other ingredients. Then make the sauce; when it boils insert the trivet, add all the browned ingredients and bring the turbigo to high pressure (15 lb). Cook for 5 minutes, reduce pressure then serve as suggested.

Family Meals

The main meal of the day, whether it is in the evening after work or at the weekend, can cause the most problems for the working wife. It is then that the well organised shopping list, storage cupboard, fridge and freezer, as well as labour-saving equipment can really come into their own.

This chapter is packed with recipes for the family to enjoy. The highlighted preparation and cooking times at the beginning of each recipe will enable you to select the recipe that will fit most easily into the time schedule for the day.

Whenever possible, take full advantage of the seasonal availability of various fruits and vegetables so that variety can be introduced into the meal as well as the correct nutrients. Working wives sometimes, however, have to save time when preparing the family meal and purchase ready-prepared dishes. Wall's are experts in supplying such products: their pies, pasties, savoury slices and flans look and taste as good as home-made. Not only are all these items available ready-baked from the grocers but they can also be purchased in bulk at freezer centres. Most of these freezer items are sold unbaked, to be baked only when required, and can therefore be eaten at their best.

A small selection of the pies available from Wall's includes Farmers' Slices (minced beef and vegetables in a light puff pastry), Chicken and Mushroom Pies (puff pastry top with chicken and mushroom in a cream sauce) and Cottage Pies (individual pies of minced beef and onion topped with creamy mashed potatoes). Any of these pies, or the flans, served to the family with either a choice of salads from pp. 61–62 or hot vegetables from pp. 52–54 would make a very appealing, nutritious and, most of all, easy meal to serve the family.

Of course, the other marvellous Wall's product to serve when time is short is Bacon Steaks. These come in packs of two, making them especially suitable for the young working wife who hasn't a family to feed at the moment. The bacon steaks can be served as simply or as elaborately as you like. Covered in parsley sauce and served with pilaf rice and a salad, they make a meal fit for a king, prepared in minutes. The recipes that begin this section show the potential of bacon steaks as main dishes when served with a delicious topping.

Apple and Cinnamon Topping
Serves 4

 PREPARATION TIME: 5 minutes

 COOKING TIMES:
Normal: 10–15 minutes
Infra-red grill: 5 minutes

☛ LABOUR-SAVING EQUIPMENT: Infra-red grill

---

4 Wall's Bacon Steaks
½ lb/225 g dessert apples, peeled and grated
1 teaspoon/5 ml spoon ground cinnamon
¼ pint/150 ml soured cream

Grill the steaks on one side for 5 minutes and then turn them over and cook the other side for 2 minutes while making the topping.

Mix the grated apple with the cinnamon and soured cream. Divide the topping between the steaks, return them to the grill and cook for a few more minutes until golden brown.

Infra-red grill Lightly oil the plates, heat and then grill the steaks for 3 minutes. Divide the topping carefully between the steaks, place the lid down again and cook for a further 2 minutes until brown.

> *Bacon steaks served with a variety of toppings: Apple and Cinnamon, Cheesy Meringue, Mustard and Sugar garnished with tomato, and parsley sauce*

Jamaican Topping
Serves 4

 PREPARATION TIME: 5 minutes

 COOKING TIMES:
Normal: 10–15 minutes
Infra-red grill: 5 minutes

☛ LABOUR-SAVING EQUIPMENT: Infra-red grill

4 Wall's Bacon Steaks
3 oz/75 g fresh breadcrumbs
1 oz/25 g walnuts, finely chopped
13½ oz/390 g can crushed pineapple, drained
1 dessertspoon/10 ml spoon honey

Grill the steaks on one side for 5 minutes and then turn them
over and grill the other side for just 2 minutes. Mix the breadcrumbs with the walnuts, pineapple and honey and divide the
topping between the steaks. Return the pan to the grill and
cook the steaks for a further 5 minutes or until they are golden
brown. Serve garnished with watercress and tomato.
Infra-red grill   Use the method given for Apple and Cinnamon
Topping above.

Mustard and Sugar Topping
Serves 1

PREPARATION TIME: 1 minute

COOKING TIME: 10 minutes

1 Wall's Bacon Steak
1 teaspoon/5 ml spoon made French mustard
1 dessertspoon/10 ml spoon demerara sugar

Grill the steak on one side for 5 minutes and then turn it over
and grill the other side for just 2 minutes. Spread the mustard
over the surface, sprinkle the sugar on top and return to the
grill to finish cooking and to allow the sugar to caramelise.

Cheesy Meringue Topping
Serves 2

 PREPARATION TIME: 5 minutes

COOKING TIME: 10–15 minutes

2 Wall's Bacon Steaks
2 oz/50 g Cheddar cheese, grated
1 egg (size 2), separated
pinch of dry mustard

Grill the steaks on one side for 5 minutes and then turn them over and grill the other side for 2 minutes. Mix the cheese with the egg yolk and mustard and divide it between the steaks. Whisk the egg white until stiff and spoon it over the cheese mixture, leaving the surface rough. Return the steaks to the grill and cook for another 5 minutes or until golden brown.

Bacon Kebabs
Serves 4

 PREPARATION TIME: 15 minutes

 COOKING TIME: 20 minutes

4 tablespoons/4 × 15 ml spoon oil
juice of ½ small lemon (approx. 1 tablespoon/15 ml spoon)
½ teaspoon/2.5 ml spoon mixed herbs
2 oz/50 g button mushrooms, trimmed
7.05 oz/200 g packet Wall's Streaky Bacon (12 rashers)
4 lamb's kidneys, skinned
2 slices of bread (1 in./2.5 cm thick) from a small loaf
1 green pepper
8 pickled onions, washed

Mix together the oil, lemon juice and herbs, add the mushrooms and leave to marinade while preparing all the other ingredients.

Cut the rind and any small bones from the bacon and stretch each rasher with the back of a knife. Wrap one around each kidney, ensuring that it is completely covered. Cut the crusts from the bread slices, cut each slice into four and again wrap a rasher of bacon around each piece. Cut the pepper in half, remove the core and seeds and cut it into eight pieces in all.

Thread the ingredients on to four skewers in the following order: bread, mushroom, pepper, onion, kidney, onion, pepper, mushroom and bread. Brush each kebab liberally with the marinade and cook under a medium grill for about 20 minutes, turning the kebabs occasionally so that they cook evenly and brushing them each time with more marinade. Serve with boiled rice and a salad.

Pan Pizza
Serves 3–4

 PREPARATION TIME: 5 minutes

 COOKING TIME: 10–15 minutes

6 oz/175 g self-raising flour
a pinch of mixed herbs
salt and pepper
4 tablespoons/4 × 15 ml spoon oil
cold water to mix
For the topping
2 tomatoes, sliced
7½ oz/215 g can sliced mushrooms in cream sauce
3 oz/85 g packet Wall's German Style Sausage (14 slices)
3 oz/75 g cheese, grated

Sift the flour and salt into a bowl, add the mixed herbs and then bind the ingredients together with 2 tablespoons/2 × 15 ml spoon oil and enough cold water to make a fairly soft mixture. Knead it lightly and roll the dough into an 8-in./20 cm round. Heat a tablespoon/15 ml spoon of the remaining oil in an 8-in./20 cm frying pan, add the dough and cook it slowly until brown underneath. Carefully turn out the dough on to a plate. Heat the remaining oil and slip the pizza base back into the pan, cooked side uppermost. Arrange the tomatoes on the cooked side with the mushrooms in cream sauce over them; overlap the sausage slices on top so that the mushroom mixture is covered and scatter over the cheese. Cook the underside of the pizza for about another 5 minutes or until brown, and then slip the frying pan under the grill to brown the cheese. Complete the dish with a green salad.

Sweet and Sour Sausages
Serves 4

 PREPARATION TIME: 10 minutes

 COOKING TIMES:
Normal: 20 minutes
Microwave oven: 15 minutes

☛ LABOUR-SAVING EQUIPMENT: Microwave oven

---

2 carrots, peeled and sliced
2 sticks celery, wiped and chopped
1 green pepper, deseeded and chopped
1 onion, peeled and chopped
2 tablespoons/2 × 15 ml spoon tomato ketchup
¼ pint/150 ml malt vinegar
2 tablespoons/2 × 15 ml spoon soy sauce
2 tablespoons/2 × 15 ml spoon clear honey
2 tablespoons/2 × 15 ml spoon cornflour
8 oz/227 g can pineapple slices
½ pint/300 ml water
1 lb/454 g packet Wall's Pork and Beef Family Size Sausages,
  cooked

Put the carrots, celery, pepper and onion into a pan, cover with water, add plenty of salt and bring to the boil. Boil for 5 minutes and then drain.

In the pan mix the tomato ketchup with the vinegar, soy sauce and honey. Blend the cornflour to a smooth paste with the juice from the pineapple. Cut the pineapple slices into pieces and add them to the pan, with the water. Bring this mixture slowly to the boil and stir a little of the hot liquid into the cornflour paste; then mix the paste into the main bulk of liquid and, stirring all the time, bring the sauce to the boil. Add the vegetables and sausages and simmer the mixture for 10–15 minutes, or until the ingredients are well blended and heated through. Serve with boiled rice and perhaps a salad.

Microwave oven Cook the carrots, onions, celery and pepper in 2 tablespoons/2 × 15 ml spoon oil at 'High' for 5 minutes and mix in the tomato ketchup, vinegar, soy sauce, and honey. Blend the cornflour to a smooth paste with the pineapple juice, chop the pineapple slices and add them to the other ingredients with the blended cornflour, sausages and hot water. Cook the dish, uncovered, for 10 minutes, stirring it once or twice to thicken the sauce.

Tomato Bacon Casserole
Serves 4

○ PREPARATION TIME: 15 minutes

● COOKING TIMES:
Normal: 1 hour 15 minutes
Automatic cooker: 1 hour 30 minutes
Pressure cooker: 20 minutes
Slow cooker: 6–10 hours

☞ LABOUR-SAVING EQUIPMENT: Automatic cooker, Pressure cooker or Slow cooker

---

1 Wall's Bacon Joint
8 oz/227 g packet Wall's Pork Chipolata Sausages
1 tablespoon/15 ml spoon oil
1 oz/25 g butter
½ lb/225 g leeks, trimmed and sliced
2 sticks celery, chopped
½ lb/225 g cooking apples, peeled, cored and thickly sliced
2 tablespoons/2 × 15 ml spoon plain flour
14 oz/400 g can tomatoes
½ pint/300 ml dry cider
pepper

Cut the bacon joint into 1 in./2.5 cm pieces and twist each sausage in half. Heat the oil and butter, add the leeks and celery and cook them gently for 5 minutes until starting to soften. Add the bacon and sausages and when the pieces are sealed stir in the apples. Mix in the flour and then stir in the tomatoes and cider. Bring the casserole to the boil, add plenty of pepper – no salt should be required – and transfer the mixture to a casserole dish. Cook at 350°F/180°C/Gas Mark 4 for 1 hour 15 minutes, adding an extra 15 minutes if using an automatic cooker.

To complete the meal, bake medium-size jacket potatoes around the dish.

Pressure cooker Prepare and fry the ingredients as described above but do not add the flour. Mix in the tomatoes and cider, bring the cooker to high pressure (15 lb) and cook for 20 minutes. Reduce the pressure and transfer the meat and vegetables to a serving dish. Blend the flour with a little water to make a smooth paste, stir in some of the hot liquid and when smooth return it to the main bulk of the liquid. Bring the sauce to the boil, stirring all the time, check for seasoning and then pour it into the serving dish. Complete the meal with plain boiled rice.

Slow cooker Prepare the casserole as for the ordinary method and then transfer it to the slow cooker. Set it at 'Low' and cook for 6–10 hours. Serve with boiled rice or creamed potatoes.

Bacon and Lentil Pot Roast
Serves 4

 PREPARATION TIME: 5–10 minutes

 COOKING TIMES:
Normal: 1½–1¾ hours
Automatic cooker: 2 hours
Pressure cooker: 20 minutes
Slow cooker: 8–10 hours

☛ LABOUR-SAVING EQUIPMENT: Automatic cooker, Pressure cooker or Slow cooker

2 onions, peeled and chopped
2 carrots, peeled and sliced
6 oz/175 g red lentils
1 Wall's Bacon Joint
½ pint/300 ml orange juice (from a carton)
¼ pint/150 ml water
pepper

Put the onions, carrots and lentils into a 3 pint/1.8 litre casserole dish and nestle the joint into the centre. Pour over the orange juice and water and season with pepper only. Cover the dish and cook the pot roast at 325°F/160°C/Gas Mark 3 for 1½–1¾ hours or until the lentils are soft. A few potatoes can be placed on the oven shelves beside the casserole to bake in their jackets at the same time, and the meal can be completed with freshly cooked cabbage.

Automatic cooker Follow the recipe above but set the auto timer for 2 hours to allow for the oven to heat up.

Pressure cooker Place all the ingredients in the cooker, cover and bring to high pressure (15 lb). Cook for 20 minutes, reduce pressure under running water and serve.

Slow cooker Place all the ingredients in the cooker, cover and cook on 'low' for 8–10 hours.

Toad-in-the-Hole
Serves 4

 PREPARATION TIME: 15 minutes

 COOKING TIME: 50 minutes

☛ LABOUR-SAVING EQUIPMENT: Liquidiser

1 lb/454 g packet Wall's Pork and Beef Thick Sausages
4 oz/100 g plain flour
salt
2 eggs (size 2)
½ teaspoon/2.5 ml spoon made English mustard
½ pint/300 ml milk

Lightly grease four shallow individual dishes or a 8 × 7 in./
20 × 18 cm roasting tin, add the sausages and cook them at
425°F/220°C/Gas Mark 7 for 10 minutes, so that they start to
brown.

Meanwhile, sift the flour and a pinch of salt into a mixing
bowl. Make a well in the centre, add the eggs and mustard and
gradually pour in the milk, stirring all the time to make a
smooth batter. Beat it for a minute to incorporate air.

When the sausages are ready pour the batter around them
and cook, still at 425°F/220°C/Gas Mark 7, for a further 30–40
minutes or until the batter is golden brown and well risen.
Serve immediately.

Liquidiser   Put the eggs for the batter into the goblet with the
flour and seasoning and half the milk, switch on the machine
and mix the ingredients together to a very thick consistency.
Gradually pour in the rest of the milk to obtain the desired
thickness. Use as previously described.

Variations

1 Cheesy batter. Beat 2 oz/50g grated cheese into the batter
mixture, pour it into the dish with the sausages and sprinkle a
further 2 oz/50 g grated cheese over the sausages before baking
as above.

2 Bacon and herb batter. Cut the rind off 7.05 oz/200 g Wall's
Streaky Bacon Rashers, stretch each with the back of a knife
and wrap each rasher around a sausage. Cook as in the original
recipe. Stir 2 teaspoons/2 × 5 ml spoon mixed herbs into the

Toad-in-the-Hole made with cheesy batter

batter, pour around the sausage and bacon corkscrews and then cook as above.

3 Tomato and onion. Cook two onions, peeled and sliced, with the sausages initially; then pour in the batter, add three tomatoes cut into quarters and cook as before.

Bacon en Croûte
Serves 4–6

 PREPARATION TIME: 15 minutes

 COOKING TIME: 30 minutes

1 oz/25 g butter
4 oz/100 g mushrooms, trimmed and sliced
4 oz/113 g packet Wall's Liver Pâté
7 oz/200 g packet frozen puff pastry, thawed
1 Wall's Bacon Joint, cooked
a little beaten egg for glaze

Melt the butter in a small pan. Add the mushrooms and cook them for about 5 minutes until tender. Beat the pâté until soft and carefully mix in the mushrooms.

On a lightly floured working surface, roll out the pastry to a 10 in./26 cm square. Trim the edges, and lift the pastry on to a baking tray. Spread half the pâté mixture in the centre, place the bacon joint on top and spread the remaining mixture on top of the joint. Moisten the pastry edges with a little egg glaze and then lift them up from corner to corner to enclose the joint, sealing it as an envelope. Scallop the edges and brush the entire pastry surface with glaze.

Bake the 'parcel' at 425°F/225°C/Gas Mark 7 for 25 minutes or until golden brown. Serve either hot or cold, cut into wedges like a cake.

Mustard-topped Liver and Bacon
Serves 4

○ PREPARATION TIME: 10 minutes

● COOKING TIMES:
Normal: 25 minutes
Microwave oven: 8–10 minutes
Pressure cooker: 7–10 minutes

☛ LABOUR-SAVING EQUIPMENT: Microwave oven or Pressure cooker

7.05 oz/200 g packet Wall's Streaky Bacon Rashers
1 tablespoon/15 ml spoon cooking oil
8 oz/225 g onions, peeled and sliced
1 lb/450 g lamb's liver, cut into strips
10½ oz/298 g can condensed oxtail soup
For the topping
6 slices French bread
1 oz/25 g butter
1 dessertspoon/10 ml spoon made English mustard

Cut the rind and any small bones from the bacon and cut each rasher into four. Fry the bacon in the oil for a few minutes; then stir in the onions and continue cooking the mixture until the onions start to soften. Add the pieces of liver and fry them until sealed, finally stirring in the soup, plus a can of water. Bring the mixture to the boil, cover and simmer for 20–25 minutes until cooked.

Spread the slices of bread with an even layer of butter and mustard. When the liver is ready, turn it into a 2–2½ pint/1.3 litre casserole dish. Arrange the bread slices on top and put the dish under a preheated grill to brown the bread. Serve the meal with creamed potatoes and buttered cabbage.

Microwave oven Put the bacon, oil, onions and liver in a glass dish, cover and microwave on 'High' for 4 minutes, stir in the soup and a can of water and microwave on 'Simmer' for 8 minutes, stirring once during cooking. Top with bread and brown under the grill as described above.

Pressure cooker Prepare as for the ordinary method but add only ½ can water. Cook at high pressure (15 lb) for 7 minutes; then reduce the pressure, turn into a casserole dish and complete as previously described.

Sausage and Bacon Pan Fry
Serves 4

PREPARATION TIME: 15 minutes

COOKING TIME: 30 minutes

You can also try this dish as part of a brunch – it makes a marvellous start to the day.

2 tablespoons/2 × 15 ml spoon oil
1 lb/454 g packet Wall's Pork Thick Sausages
2 large onions, peeled and sliced
7.05 oz/200 g packet Wall's Streaky Bacon Rashers
1 lb/450 g potatoes, peeled and parboiled
grated rind and juice of ½ lemon
salt and black pepper
chopped parsley to garnish

Fry the sausage in 1 tablespoon/15 ml spoon oil until golden brown and cooked. Transfer to a plate and keep warm. Wipe out the frying pan, heat the rest of the oil and fry the onions gently until almost cooked. Cut the rashers into fours, add to the onion and cook for a few minutes; then slice the potatoes and add them to the pan. Very carefully, turning the mixture occasionally, cook these ingredients together until the potato is brown (about 10 minutes). Cut each sausage diagonally into three, add to the pan with the lemon rind and juice, season well and when the flavours are well distributed sprinkle the dish with parsley and serve with a tomato and chive salad.

Sausage and Bacon Pan Fry

Sausage Pie
Serves 4

○ PREPARATION TIME: 15 minutes

● COOKING TIMES:
Normal: 45 minutes
Automatic cooker: 1 hour

☞ LABOUR-SAVING EQUIPMENT: Automatic cooker

1 lb/454 g packet Wall's Pork and Beef Thick Sausages, cooked
and chopped
8 oz/225 g green beans, cooked
10½ oz/298 g can condensed mushroom soup
14 oz/400 g packet frozen puff pastry, thawed
1 egg, beaten, to glaze

Mix the sausage, beans and soup together and turn them into a
2 pint/1.2 litre pie dish.

Roll out the pastry to cover the pie, using the trimmings for
decoration, and glaze with the beaten egg. Place the dish on a
baking sheet and cook at 400°F/200°C/Gas Mark 6 for 45
minutes (1 hour if using an automatic cooker). Complete the
meal with creamed or jacket potatoes and a green vegetable,
such as cabbage.

Sausage and Potato Bake
Serves 4

○ PREPARATION TIME: 10 minutes

● COOKING TIMES:
Normal: 45 minutes
Automatic cooker: 1 hour

☞ LABOUR-SAVING EQUIPMENT: Automatic cooker

7 oz/200 g can corn niblets, drained
2 tablespoons/2 × 15 ml spoon salad cream
½ lb/225 g tomatoes, sliced
2 lb/1 kg potatoes, peeled, cooked and sliced
1 lb/454 g packet Wall's Pork with Herb Thick Sausages
7.05 oz/200 g packet Wall's Streaky Bacon Rashers
2 oz/50 g cheese, grated

Thickly butter a 3 pint/1.8 litre ovenproof dish. Mix the corn niblets and salad cream together and spread in the bottom of the dish. Arrange the tomatoes over the mixture and the potatoes, slightly overlapping, over the tomatoes. Separate the sausages and cut the rind and any small bones from the bacon. Wrap a rasher of bacon around each sausage and place them, with the bacon joins underneath, down the centre of the dish on top of the potatoes. Finally chop the one remaining rasher, mix it with the cheese and scatter over the sausages.

Bake the dish at 375°F/190°C/Gas Mark 5 for 45 minutes; add an extra 15 minutes to the cooking time if the cooker is left on automatic. Complete the meal with a green salad.

Sausages Supreme
Serves 4

 PREPARATION TIME: 10 minutes

 COOKING TIME: 15 minutes

1 lb/454 g packet Wall's Pork Thick Sausages
1½ lb/750 g potatoes, peeled, cooked and creamed with milk and butter
1 tablespoon/15 ml spoon cornflour
1 dessertspoon/10 ml spoon malt vinegar
¼ pint/150 ml beef stock
1 tablespoon/15 ml spoon redcurrant jelly
1 tablespoon/15 ml spoon sweet chutney
½ teaspoon/2.5 ml spoon paprika pepper
1 teaspoon/5 ml spoon soy sauce
chopped parsley to garnish

Fry or grill the sausages until evenly brown and cooked. Fork or pipe the potatoes around the edge of an oval serving dish or four individual dishes. Place under the grill to brown.

Meanwhile, to make the sauce, blend the cornflour and mustard to a smooth paste in a pan with the vinegar and a little of the stock and then mix in the redcurrant jelly, chutney, paprika pepper, soy sauce and the rest of the stock. Stirring all the time, bring the sauce to the boil and cook it for a few minutes to thicken. Place the sausages in the centre of the potatoes, pour over the sauce and garnish with a little parsley. Serve with either a salad or a green vegetable such as peas or French beans.

Sausage Hot Pot
Serves 4

PREPARATION TIME: 15 minutes

COOKING TIMES:
Normal: 1¼ hours
Automatic cooker: 1½ hours

☞ LABOUR-SAVING EQUIPMENT: Automatic cooker

1 lb/454 g packet Wall's Pork with Herb Thick Sausages
1 tablespoon/15 ml spoon oil
¾ lb/350 g onions, peeled and sliced
2 sticks celery, wiped and chopped
1 lb/450 g carrots, peeled and sliced
salt and pepper
½ pint/300 ml beef stock
2 teaspoons/2 × 5 ml spoon Worcestershire sauce
1 teaspoon/5 ml spoon mixed herbs
pinch of garlic salt (optional)
1 oz/25 g butter
1 lb/450 g potatoes, peeled and thinly sliced

Quickly and lightly brown the sausages in the oil and transfer them to a plate. Add the onions to the pan and when they are soft, but not brown, mix in the celery and carrots and cook the vegetables together for a few minutes. Sprinkle the mixture with salt and pepper and turn half of it into a 4 pint/2.5 litre casserole dish. Add the sausages and then the rest of the vegetable mixture to the casserole.

Mix the stock with the Worcestershire sauce, herbs and garlic salt and pour it into the dish. Overlap the sliced potatoes on top, dot with butter and bake at 400°F/200°C/Gas Mark 6 for 1¼ hours.

Automatic cooker Follow the above recipe but melt the butter and brush it thoroughly over the potatoes, so that they do not blacken while waiting in the oven. Increase the cooking time to 1½ hours to allow for the cold start.

Spicy Sausage Pilaf
Serves 4–6

 PREPARATION TIME: 10 minutes

 COOKING TIME: 30 minutes

☞ LABOUR-SAVING EQUIPMENT: Microwave oven

1 lb/454 g packet Wall's Pork Family Size Sausages, cooked
2 tablespoons/2 × 15 ml spoon oil
8 oz/225 g onion, peeled and chopped
8 oz/225 g long-grain rice
1 tablespoon/15 ml spoon curry powder
1 teaspoon/5 ml spoon ground ginger
½ teaspoon/2.5 ml spoon chilli seasoning
½ teaspoon/2.5 ml spoon ground cloves
pinch of garlic salt
2 tablespoons/2 × 15 ml spoon tomato purée
2 tablespoons/2 × 15 ml spoon malt vinegar
1 tablespoon/15 ml spoon Worcestershire sauce
1½ pints/900 ml stock
1 oz/25 g salted peanuts

Chop each sausage into four and leave on one side.

Heat the oil in a covered frying pan; add the onions and fry them for 5 minutes or until starting to soften but not brown. Stir in the rice, curry powder, ginger, chilli, cloves, garlic salt, tomato purée, vinegar and Worcestershire sauce and when they are well blended mix in the stock. Slowly bring the liquid to the boil and then add the sausage pieces. Cover the pan and simmer the mixture for 25–30 minutes, or until the rice is soft to the centre and has absorbed all the liquid. Adjust the seasoning, scatter with peanuts and serve accompanied by tomato and green salads.

Microwave oven   Cook the onions and oil together on 'High' for 5 minutes. Add all the other ingredients (using hot stock), stir them well and cook for 20 minutes more, stirring the mixture occasionally, until almost all the water has been absorbed. Leave the dish, covered, on one side for 5 minutes and then serve as suggested above.

Bacon Bonus
Serves 4

PREPARATION TIME: 15 minutes, including night before

COOKING TIMES:
Normal: 3 hours
Automatic cooker: 3¼ hours
Pressure cooker: 20 minutes
Slow cooker: 10–12 hours

☞ LABOUR-SAVING EQUIPMENT: Automatic cooker, Pressure cooker or Slow cooker

---

4 oz/100 g butter beans
¾ pint/450 ml apple juice
3 sticks celery, trimmed and chopped
2 leeks, cleaned and sliced
6 oz/175 g swede, peeled and cut into ½ in./1 cm pieces
6 oz/175 g parsnip, peeled and cut into 1 in./1 cm pieces
6 oz/175 g turnip, peeled and cut into ½ in./1 cm pieces
2 carrots, peeled and sliced
1 Wall's Bacon Joint
1 teaspoon/5 ml spoon dried basil
pepper and salt

Put the butter beans into a 4 pint/2.5 litre casserole dish, pour over the apple juice and leave them overnight to soak.

Next day, add the prepared celery, leeks, swede, parsnip, turnip and carrots. Nestle the bacon joint in the centre and sprinkle over the basil. Cover the dish and cook the meal at 325°F/160°C/Gas Mark 3 for 3 hours or until all the ingredients are tender. Check for seasoning, then serve with Brussels sprouts and creamed potatoes.

Automatic cooker Follow the recipe above, leaving the prepared meal in the oven before going to work. Set the auto timer at 325°F/160°C/Gas Mark 3 to cook for 3¼ hours. Complete the meal as suggested.

Pressure cooker Either leave the beans to soak in the apple juice overnight or, if you leave the preparation of the meal until you return home from work, place the beans in a bowl, pour over sufficient boiling water to cover and leave on one side, covered, while preparing the other ingredients. Place them all in the pressure cooker, pour over the apple juice and add the drained butter beans and basil. Cover the cooker and bring it to high pressure – 15 lb. Cook for 20 minutes, reduce the pressure under cold, running water and serve.

Slow cooker Soak the beans in the apple juice overnight. Next day, add all the ingredients, cover the cooker and cook on 'Low' for 10–12 hours.

Bacon Fricassée
Serves 4–6

 PREPARATION TIME: 5 minutes

 COOKING TIME: 20 minutes

2 oz/50 g butter
2 oz/50 g plain flour
½ pint/300 ml milk
¼ pint/150 ml dry cider
grated rind and juice of 1 small lemon
1 Wall's Bacon Joint, cooked and cut into cubes
pepper
2 rashers Wall's Streaky Bacon, grilled, to garnish
chopped parsley to garnish

Melt the butter in a pan, stir in the flour and then, off the heat, gradually blend in the milk and cider to make a smooth consistency. Return the pan to the heat and, stirring all the time, bring the sauce to the boil to thicken. Stir in the lemon rind and juice and cubes of bacon joint, season to taste and simmer the fricassée for 10 minutes so that it is thoroughly heated. Garnish with the grilled bacon and parsley.

Bacon Fricassée

A VARIETY OF VEGETABLES

When you are a working wife it is sometimes difficult to resist the temptation to fall back on frozen vegetables to accompany the meal, just for the sheer speed and convenience. I can't claim that the following recipes are as quick to prepare and easy to cook as a packet of frozen peas, but they will certainly add extra taste and nutrition to the meal.

Cheesy Potatoes
Serves 4–6

 PREPARATION TIME: 10 minutes

 COOKING TIME: 10–15 minutes

1½ lb/750 g potatoes, peeled and cooked
1 oz/25 g margarine
1 oz/25 g plain flour
¾ pint/450 ml milk
4 oz/100 g Cheddar cheese, grated
a pinch of dry mustard powder
a pinch of cayenne

Cut the potatoes into 1 in./2.5 cm pieces and put them into an ovenproof dish. Put the margarine, flour and milk into a pan and slowly bring to the boil, whisking all the time until the sauce is smooth and thickened. Stir in almost all the cheese, the mustard and cayenne and adjust the sauce for seasoning. Pour it over the potatoes and sprinkle the remaining cheese over the top. Place the dish under a preheated grill and cook for 10–15 minutes until thoroughly hot and brown and bubbling.

Glazed Carrots
Serves 4–6

 PREPARATION TIME: 10 minutes

 COOKING TIME: 20 minutes

1 oz/25 g margarine
1 tablespoon/15 ml spoon oil
1 medium onion, peeled and chopped
1½ lb/750 g carrots, peeled and sliced (see note below)
1 tablespoon/15 ml spoon demerara sugar
1 tablespoon/15 ml spoon water
a little freshly chopped parsley to garnish

Put the magarine and oil into a pan and add the onion, carrots, sugar and water, with plenty of seasoning. Cover the pan and cook over a medium heat for 15 minutes or until almost tender. Remove the lid, stir and then cook uncovered for the last 5 minutes to evaporate any excess liquid. Turn the carrots into a serving dish and sprinkle with parsley before serving.
Note: If small, new carrots are used, simply scrape them and cook them whole.

Crunchy Cabbage
Serves 4–6

PREPARATION TIME: 10 minutes

COOKING TIME: 40 minutes

1½ lb/750 g white cabbage
2 tablespoons/2 × 15 ml spoon oil
4 oz/100 g Wall's Streaky Bacon Rashers
1 large onion, peeled and chopped
a pinch of nutmeg
4 oz/25 g sultanas
1 oz/25 g salted peanuts to garnish

Trim and shred the cabbage. Heat the oil in a large pan. Cut the rind and any small bones from the bacon and cut the rashers into small pieces. Add them to the oil with the onion and fry the two together until starting to soften. Stir in the cabbage, nutmeg and plenty of seasoning. Cover the pan and cook the vegetables over a medium heat for 20 minutes, stirring them occasionally so they do not stick. Add the sultanas and cook the mixture, still covered, for a further 20 minutes or until tender. Serve sprinkled with peanuts.

Vegetable Medley
Serves 4

 PREPARATION TIME: 10 minutes

 COOKING TIME: 2–2½ hours

This vegetable dish is very easy to prepare and makes an ideal accompaniment to a casserole cooking in an automatic oven (see the Special Occasion menu on pp. 84–86).

1 small (1½ lb/750 g) marrow
1 oz/25 g butter
2 medium onions, peeled and chopped
2 sticks celery, washed, trimmed and chopped
3 tomatoes, skinned and chopped
a sprig of thyme

Peel the marrow, remove the seeds and cut into 1 in./2.5 cm pieces. Grease a casserole dish with half the butter and add all the vegetables, stirring them together so that they are thoroughly mixed. Sprinkle liberally with salt and pepper, dot the rest of the butter on top and nestle the sprig of thyme in the centre. Cover the dish and cook at 350°F/180°C/Gas Mark 4 for 2–2½ hours. It will reduce in bulk greatly during cooking, so it may look nicer if transferred to a smaller serving dish before putting it on the table.

Super Snacks, Salads and Packed Lunches

Almost every recipe in this chapter has more than one use. Snack ideas are always so versatile they also make delicious lunches and suppers, and some could even be taken as part of a packed lunch. For the busy wife, snack recipes are ideal – if members of the family tend to eat their meals at different times then each portion can be cooked when required and served fresh and piping hot.

Wall's produce a vast range of foods perfect for quick snacks or packed lunches. A pork pie, a selection of cold meats or perhaps a flan will make an instant but very tasty meal, especially if completed with one of the interesting salad recipes to be found on pp. 61–62. In the Wall's cold pie range there is a pork pie to suit almost everyone's tastes – party pies are small and perfect for the children, the larger pies are ideal for adults and the Melton Mowbray pies are a favourite with those who like uncured meat.

The flans, in either individual or family sizes, can be purchased from the chilled cabinet at your local grocer's or in bulk from a home freezer store. There are several different fillings in the range – Egg Bacon and Cheese, Ham and Pepper or Mushroom, Egg, Bacon and Cheese – all of which should be heated through in the oven for a few minutes.

More and more children are taking packed lunches to school these days, and the possibilities offered here by the Wall's cold eating range should not be overlooked. Items such as Scotch Eggs and Cornish Pasties are ideal for making up varied and interesting lunches; they also transport easily – quite important if the lunch box is swung about on its journey to school!

Suggested Five-day Packed Lunch Menu

Monday	2 Wall's sausage rolls, tomato, banana or orange, bar of chocolate.
Tuesday	Bacon and Cheese Sandwich (see p. 72), stick of celery, apple, slice of fruit cake.
Wednesday	Wall's Pork Pie, piece of cucumber, packet of crisps, pear, 2 sweet biscuits.
Thursday	Sausage and Peanut Butter Sandwich (see p. 72) peeled raw carrot, yogurt, apple, chocolate wafer biscuit.
Friday	Wall's Cornish Pasty, tomato, piece of sponge cake, small packet of seedless raisins, orange.

Accompany each menu with a drink if this is not available at the school. I would suggest a flask of warm, milk-based drink, such as hot chocolate, or a soup in the winter; in the summer you could pack a long cool drink, like lemon barley water or blackcurrant.

Seashore Toasts
Serves 4

 PREPARATION TIME: 10 minutes

 COOKING TIME: 25 minutes

4 slices bread
1 oz/25 g butter
7½ oz/210 g can tomatoes
4 oz/100 g Cheddar cheese, grated
3½ oz/100 g can tuna fish, drained
4 rashers Wall's Streaky Bacon

Spread the bread with the butter and place it buttered side down on a baking tray. Drain the tomatoes (reserving the juice to add to a casserole, soup or stock), mix them with the cheese and tuna fish and spread this topping evenly over the bread. Cut the rind from the bacon, cut each rasher in half lengthways and arrange in a cross over the filling. Bake the toasts at 375°F/190°C/Gas Mark 5 for 20–25 minutes or until brown.

Sausage Top Hats
Makes 6

 PREPARATION TIME: 5 minutes

 COOKING TIME: 15 minutes

6 round slices bread
1½ oz/40 g butter
7½ oz/213 g packet Wall's Beef Sausage Slices
3 teaspoons/3 × 5 ml spoon made French mustard or brown
 sauce
2 tomatoes, sliced
3 oz/75 g grated cheese

Spread the bread with the butter and place the slices butter side down into a shallow baking tin. Spread the bread with the mustard (children may prefer the brown sauce) and put a slice of beef sausage on top of each slice of bread, not forgetting to remove the casing from the sausage. Next comes a slice of tomato and, finally, a sprinkling of cheese. Bake at 400°F/200°C/Gas Mark 6 for 15 minutes or until golden brown. Serve garnished with watercress.

Ham and Banana Rolls
Serves 3–4

PREPARATION TIME: 5 minutes

COOKING TIME: 10–15 minutes

2 × 3 oz/85 g packet Wall's Choice Ham (8 slices)
4 bananas
10½ oz/298 g can condensed celery soup
2 tablespoons/2 × 15 ml spoon milk
1 oz/25 g cheese, grated
1 tablespoon/15 ml spoon rolled porridge oats

Peel and cut the bananas in half lengthways and wrap a slice of ham around each half. Arrange them in a shallow ovenproof dish. Heat the soup with the milk, spoon it over the bananas and sprinkle over the cheese and oats mixed together. Place the dish under a preheated grill and cook for 10–15 minutes until golden brown and bubbling. Garnish with watercress and serve with freshly made toast.

Glazed Sausages
Serves 4–6

○ PREPARATION TIME: 3 minutes

● COOKING TIME: 10–15 minutes

Here are two ways of just adding that little extra to any of the
sausages in the Wall's range. They are delicious served either
hot or cold, and make a tasty addition to a packed lunch.

Chilli Sausages
1 teaspoon/5 ml spoon chilli powder
1 tablespoon/15 ml spoon tomato ketchup
½ teaspoon/2.5 ml spoon paprika pepper
1 small onion, peeled and finely grated
1 lb/454 g packet Wall's Pork Thick Sausages

Mix the chilli powder, tomato ketchup, paprika pepper and
onion together. Separate the sausages and place them into the
grill pan, removing the rack. Brush the glaze mixture over the
sausages and then grill them for 10–15 minutes, or until golden
brown and cooked. Turn the sausages frequently as they cook,
basting them each time with more of the glaze, so that the
flavour really penetrates. Serve hot or cold.

Curried Sausages
2 teaspoons/2 × 5 ml spoon curry paste
2 teaspoons/2 × 5 ml spoon apricot jam
1 teaspoon/5 ml spoon lemon juice
¼ teaspoon/1.25 ml spoon ground coriander
1 lb/454 g packet Wall's Pork and Beef Thick Sausages

Mix the curry paste, apricot jam, lemon juice and coriander
together then glaze and cook as for Chilli Sausages above.

*Picnic fare: a choice of sliced ham, Scotch eggs, pies and pasties with
Glazed Sausages and Bacon and Cheese Sandwich (see p. 72)*

Thick Winter Soup
Serves 4–6

○ PREPARATION TIME: 10 minutes, plus soaking peas overnight

● COOKING TIMES:
Normal: 1½–2 hours
Slow cooker: 10–12 hours

☛ LABOUR-SAVING EQUIPMENT: Slow cooker

A bowl of hot soup thick with meat and vegetables is always welcomed by the family. It can either be served as a first course, with perhaps cold meat and salads to follow, or as a supper dish with fresh crusty bread.

4 oz/100 g split peas
4 oz/100 g Wall's Streaky Bacon Rashers
1 large onion, peeled and chopped
6 oz/175 g packet Wall's Polony
4 oz/100 g sweetcorn kernels, cooked
1 tablespoon/15 ml spoon cornflour
1½ pints/900 ml chicken stock
1 bay leaf
1 tablespoon/15 ml spoon chopped parsley

Put the peas into a bowl, pour over enough boiling water to cover and leave overnight to soak.

Next day cut the rind and any small bones from the bacon and chop the rashers into small pieces; fry them over a medium heat until the fat starts to run. Add the onion and cook the two ingredients together until the onion starts to soften. Cut the polony into small dice and add the pieces to the pan with the sweetcorn. Blend the cornflour to a smooth paste with a little of the chicken stock and mix it into the other ingredients with the rest of the stock. Stirring all the time, bring the soup to the boil. Then reduce the heat, add the bay leaf, cover the pan and simmer the soup for 1½–2 hours, stirring it occasionally until all the ingredients are cooked. Sprinkle with chopped parsley before serving.
Slow cooker Follow the instructions for the conventional method of cooking; when the soup has come to the boil transfer it to the slow cooker and cook on 'Low' for 10–12 hours.

A SELECTION OF SALADS

For a really instant lunch or supper serve a pork pie, a selection of cold meats or a flan from the vast range of Wall's products and complete the meal with one of these interesting salads.

Watercress Salad
Serves 3–4

 PREPARATION TIME: 5 minutes

1 bunch watercress
1 large carrot, peeled and coarsely grated
2 tomatoes, each cut into eight
2 tablespoons/2 × 5 ml spoon salad oil
1 tablespoon/15 ml spoon vinegar
1 dessertspoon/10 ml spoon tomato ketchup
salt and pepper
½ teaspoon/2.5 ml spoon caster sugar
4 oz/113 g carton cottage cheese

Wash and trim the watercress and put it into a bowl; stir in the grated carrot and tomato pieces. Put the oil, vinegar, tomato ketchup, seasoning and sugar into a screw-topped jar, cover and shake together. Pour the dressing over the salad ingredients and toss them until thoroughly coated. Turn out the salad on to a serving dish and spoon the cottage cheese into the centre before serving.

Bean Sprout Salad
Serves 4

 PREPARATION TIME: 10 minutes

10 oz/275 g fresh bean sprouts
4 oz/100 g button mushrooms, trimmed and quartered
8 oz/225 g frozen sweetcorn, cooked
12 sprigs fresh parsley
¼ pint/150 ml soured cream
1 tablespoon/15 ml spoon malt vinegar
1 tablespoon/15 ml spoon soy sauce
1 teaspoon/5 ml spoon sugar
salt and pepper
4 rashers Wall's Streaky Bacon, fried or grilled

Mix the bean sprouts with the mushrooms, sweetcorn and parsley. Put the soured cream into a jar, add the vinegar, soy sauce, sugar and seasoning and shake them all together. Pour the dressing over the salad and toss the ingredients so that they are completely coated.

Turn the salad into a serving bowl. Cut the cooked bacon rashers into pieces and scatter them over the surface before serving.

Red Bean Salad
Serves 4

 PREPARATION TIME: 10 minutes

☛ **LABOUR-SAVING EQUIPMENT:** Liquidiser

15 oz/425 g can red kidney beans
½ cucumber
3 sticks celery
1 green-skinned apple, cored and sliced
1 oz/25 g cleaned raisins
1 tablespoon/15 ml spoon vinegar
3 tablespoons/3 × 15 ml spoon oil
1 oz/25 g walnut pieces
1 teaspoon/5 ml spoon granulated sugar
½ teaspoon/2.5 ml spoon made French mustard

Drain and rinse the beans and put them into a bowl. Cut the cucumber into small dice, keeping the skin on if preferred, and mix it into the beans. Trim and chop the celery and stir it in, together with the apple and raisins.

Put all the remaining ingredients into the liquidiser and switch the machine on for a few minutes until they are emulsified. Pour the dressing into the bowl and toss the salad thoroughly before serving.

Note: If no liquidiser is available chop the nuts finely and shake all the ingredients for the dressing together in a screw-topped jar.

Bean Sprout Salad and Watercress Salad are ideal accompaniments to pork pies and savoury flans for a cold lunch

HOT SANDWICHES

A hot sandwich, fried, toasted or cooked in an infra-red grill, makes a quick and delicious snack. Serve the sandwich as soon as possible after cooking, garnished with cucumber, tomato and perhaps a little watercress.

Here are just a few variations, although obviously the combinations of flavours are limitless.

Each sandwich serves 1

 PREPARATION TIME: 5 minutes

 COOKING TIMES:
Normal: 5 minutes
Infra-red grill: 3 minutes

☛ LABOUR-SAVING EQUIPMENT: Infra-red grill

Ham and Cheese Sandwich
2 slices bread, buttered
1 oz/25 g cheese, sliced
1 slice Wall's Choice Cooked Shoulder
1 oz/25 g butter
1 tablespoon/15 ml spoon oil

Make a sandwich with the bread, cheese and cooked shoulder. Heat the butter and oil in the frying pan, add the sandwich and fry for about 5 minutes, turning it halfway through the cooking time so that it browns on both sides.
Infra-red grill Make the sandwich as above, spread the outside of the bread with the butter (omit the oil) and then cook between the heated plates for about 3 minutes or until golden brown.

Bacon and Tomato Sandwich
2 rashers Wall's Back Bacon
2 slices bread, buttered
1 tomato, thinly sliced
1 tablespoon/15 ml spoon oil

Cut the rind from the bacon and fry the rashers until just cooked. Make a sandwich with the bread, cooked bacon and sliced tomatoes. Heat the oil in the pan with any remaining bacon fat and quickly fry the sandwich on both sides until golden brown and crispy – about 5 minutes in all.

Infra-red Grill Cook the bacon between the heated plates until tender and make up the sandwich. Brush the cooker plates carefully with the oil and cook the sandwich for about 3 minutes or until golden brown.

Luncheon Meat and Coleslaw Sandwich

2 slices bread
½ oz/15 g butter
2 lettuce leaves
2 slices Wall's Pork Luncheon Meat
2 oz/50 g coleslaw salad

Toast the bread on both sides and spread with butter. Cover one slice of bread with lettuce and then luncheon meat. Put the coleslaw on top of this and make into a toasted sandwich. Cut in half and serve immediately.

Infra-red grill Using untoasted bread, butter it then make the sandwich as previously described, omitting the lettuce. Lightly grease the heated plates of the infra-red grill and cook the sandwich for about 3 minutes until golden brown. Add the lettuce and serve.

Sausage and Chutney Sandwich

2 slices bread
½ oz/15 g butter
2 Wall's Pork Sausages, freshly cooked and sliced
1 tablespoon/15 ml spoon sweet chutney

Toast the bread on both sides, spread with butter and then cover one slice with chutney. Arrange the sliced sausages on top, cover with the other piece of buttered toast, cut in half and serve immediately.

Infra-red grill Butter the untoasted bread and make up the sandwich. Brush the heated plates of the infra-red grill with a little oil and cook the sandwich for about 3 minutes or until golden brown.

Children's Favourites

As children are always 'starving' when they come home from school, the following recipes will prove a success with the working mum as well as the hungry children. I have included two fun ideas for tea that are very quick to prepare and much appreciated if your children bring friends home after school.

There may be times when the older children arrive home before you, and could cook something for themselves. The recipes marked with a ☆ are those that I consider could be cooked with safety unsupervised; obviously, the final decision must rest with you. An alternative is just to leave some cold cooked sausages in the fridge. You will find Wall's skinless sausages very popular with young and old alike: they are a very convenient size and so easy to eat that they disappear quicker than you expect. With some rolls left in the bread bin, they make a tasty stop-gap to sustain your children until you arrive home to cook the tea.

Fun recipes for children – Sausage Castle and The Sausage Express

Sausage Castle
Serves 4–6

 PREPARATION TIME: 5 minutes

 COOKING TIME: 25 minutes

Presentation of food is always so important with children and this 'castle' is ideal for a busy Mum who finds she has to entertain her children's friends for tea. Basically, it is only sausages and mash – but you will find the children will adore it.

2 × 7½ oz/213 g packets Wall's Pork Skinless Sausages
1 oz/25 g butter
2 tablespoons/2 × 15 ml spoon milk
1½ lb/750 g potatoes, peeled, cooked and mashed
8 oz/225 g frozen peas

Grill or fry the sausages until golden brown and cooked. Beat the butter and milk into the mashed potato and then pile it on to the centre of a plate. Shape it into a mound about 5 in./13 cm in diameter. Stand the sausages up against the sides to form the walls of the castle. Cook the peas and spoon them around the edge for the moat. If possible, complete the dish with a flag placed on top of the potatoes and a few toy soldiers around the base!

The Sausage Express
Serves 4

 PREPARATION TIME: 5 minutes

1 pack of 6 small Wall's Sausage Rolls
4 Hovis rolls
2 oz/50 g butter
15 oz/425 g can beans in tomato sauce
1 carrot, peeled

Warm the sausage rolls in a moderate oven. Meanwhile, cut off the tops of the Hovis rolls and scoop out the bread from the centres; spread butter around the inside of each. Warm the beans.

Now assemble the train. On a long board or tray place 2 sausage rolls end to end for the engine with 2 more, one on top of the other, for the cab. Divide the baked beans between the rolls piling the 'cargo' high and place them in a line behind the engine for trucks. Cut 6 thick slices from the carrot to form the wheels of the engine and balance the pointed ends on top for the funnels. Finally, cut each of the remaining 2 sausage rolls carefully into 4 slices and place these in position for the truck wheels. 'All aboard'!

Battered Bangers
Serves 4–6

 PREPARATION TIME: 5 minutes

 COOKING TIME: 20 minutes

A real favourite with the children, but the cooking must be left to Mum.

4 oz/100 g plain flour
½ teaspoon/2.5 ml spoon dry mustard powder
salt and pepper
1 tablespoon/15 ml spoon oil
1 egg (size 3)
¼ pint/150 ml milk
2 × 7½ oz/213 g packets Wall's Pork and Beef Skinless
    Sausages
a little extra flour
deep fat for frying

Put the 4 oz/100 g flour into a bowl with the mustard and seasoning and make a well in the centre. Pour in the oil, break in the egg and gradually mix in the flour, at the same time adding the milk to make a smooth batter.

Heat the deep fat pan until a piece of bread slipped into the fat browns in about a minute. Dust the sausages in the extra flour, dip each into the batter and then cook in the fat for about 5 minutes or until golden brown and puffy. It is best to cook only three or four at a time; do not use the basket as the sausages tend to stick to it. Drain on absorbent paper and keep warm while cooking the rest. Serve with chips or a coleslaw salad.

Spaghetti and Sausage Sizzle ☆
Serves 4–6

 PREPARATION TIME: 5 minutes

 COOKING TIMES:
Normal: 10 minutes
Microwave oven: 5 minutes

☛ LABOUR-SAVING EQUIPMENT: Microwave oven

1 medium onion, peeled and sliced
1 tablespoon/15 ml spoon oil
6 Wall's Pork and Beef Thick Sausages, cooked and chopped
2 × 15 oz/425 g can Alphabet Spaghetti
salt and pepper
chopped parsley
triangles of toast

Fry the onion gently in the oil until cooked. Add the chopped sausages and the spaghetti. Season and then heat the mixture thoroughly. Just before serving, sprinkle over the chopped parsley and add the toast triangles.
Microwave oven Put the onion and oil into a shallow dish, cover and cook for 2 minutes. Stir in the spaghetti and chopped sausages and cook, covered again, for a further 3–5 minutes, stirring once more if necessary.

Fish Finger Corkscrews ☆
Serves 3–4

 PREPARATION TIME: 5 minutes

 COOKING TIME: 5–10 minutes

8 fish fingers
4 rashers Wall's Streaky Bacon

Cut the rind and any small bones from the bacon and with the back of the knife stretch each rasher to almost twice its length. Cut the rashers in half, wrap a piece around each fish finger and place on a grill pan with the ends underneath. Grill the

corkscrews for 5–10 minutes, turning them halfway through the cooking time so they brown and cook evenly. Serve with chips or baked beans.

Fillings for Sandwiches and Rolls

Sandwiches or filled rolls are always a firm favourite with children and, of course, they are ideal for the working mum, as they can be left all ready for the children on their return from school. Alternatively some of these ideas can be used as a basis for packed lunches.

Each filling is sufficient for 2 slices of buttered bread (1 complete sandwich) or 2 buttered rolls.

Sausage and Peanut Butter
1 Wall's Pork Thick Sausage, cooked
1 tablespoon/15 ml spoon peanut butter
1 small tomato, sliced
Cut the sausage into four slices lengthways. Spread the bread or rolls with peanut butter and arrange the sausage and tomato slices on top. Cover, press down and cut into desired shape.

Bacon and Cheese
2 rashers Wall's Back Bacon, cooked and chopped
1 tablespoon/15 ml spoon coleslaw
1 tablespoon/15 ml spoon grated cheese
Mix together the bacon, salad and cheese, and lay on the bread or use to fill the rolls. Cover, press down and cut.

Tasty Pork and Ham
2 slices Wall's Chopped Pork and Ham
1 cold cooked potato, thinly sliced
1 dessertspoon/10 ml spoon sweet chutney
Spread the chutney on the bread or rolls and place the chopped pork and ham and potato on top. Cover, press down and cut.

Sausage and Cucumber
1 Wall's Pork Thick Sausage, cooked
6 slices cucumber
1 dessertspoon/10 ml spoon salad cream
Cut the sausage into four slices lengthways, spread the salad cream over the bread or rolls and complete with the sliced sausage and cucumber. Cover, press down and cut.

Delicious Desserts

When time is at a premium when preparing the main meal of the day it is often the dessert that gets overlooked or replaced by cheese and fruit. Although both cheese and fruit are very nutritious, and can be varied each day with the vast selection available, many people (especially the youngsters in the family) hanker after a sweet dessert of some sort. This is where, for the working wife, Wall's ice cream fits into the menu perfectly.

The choice of flavours, shapes and colours is enormous and, with stockists throughout the country, Wall's ice creams are readily available to everyone. Nothing could be easier to prepare than a few scoops of Golden Vanilla in a dish, topped with either a sauce from the Wall's range of dessert sauces – strawberry, raspberry or chocolate – or one of your own home-made sauces. All these sauces keep well in a cool place.

Baked Alaska
Serves 6

Ⓞ PREPARATION TIME: 5–10 minutes

Ⓞ COOKING TIME: 3–5 minutes

3 trifle sponges or a piece of sponge cake a little larger than a
    family-size ice cream block
2 tablespoons/2 × 15 ml spoon orange juice
½ lb/225 g fresh fruit (e.g. strawberries, bananas, oranges,
    peaches) or 15 oz/425 g can of fruit
3 egg whites (size 2)
6 oz/175 g caster sugar
1 Family Block Wall's Raspberry Ripple ice cream

Put the sponge on an ovenproof plate and soak it with the
orange juice. (If canned fruit is used, use the syrup to soak the
sponge and omit the orange juice.) Prepare the fruit, if using
fresh fruit, and place it on top of the sponge. Set aside in a cool
place until needed.

Whisk the egg whites until really stiff and standing in
straight peaks. Add 3 tablespoons/3 × 15 ml spoon sugar from
the measured amount and re-whisk until the meringue regains
its original stiffness; then carefully fold in the remaining sugar.
Place the ice cream on top of the fruit-covered sponge and
cover it *completely* with the meringue (this is the secret of a
successful Baked Alaska – if any ice cream shows through the
meringue then it will be exposed to the heat and therefore
melt).

Bake the Alaska immediately at 450°F/230°C/Gas Mark 8 for
3–5 minutes or until tinged golden brown.

Baked Alaska

Ice Cream Cassata
Serves 6

 PREPARATION TIME: 15 minutes

½ litre Wall's Soft Scoop Golden Vanilla ice cream
⅓ litre Wall's Italiano Rich Toffee ice cream
¼ litre Wall's Soft Scoop Tutti Frutti ice cream
butterscotch sauce (optional: for recipe, see p. 78)

Spoon the vanilla ice cream into a 1½ pint/900 ml pudding basin and, using the back of a wet tablespoon, spread it over the base and up the sides so that the basin is evenly coated. Place the basin in the freezer for 5 minutes to re-harden and then repeat the process, using Rich Toffee for the second layer. Chill again for 5 minutes and finally fill the centre with Tutti Frutti. Smooth the surface level and store in the freezer until required.

To serve, dip the bowl into hot water for a quick count of 3 and then invert it on to a plate. Cut into wedges and complete with the butterscotch sauce, if required.

Ice Cream Brûlée
Serves 4–6

 PREPARATION TIME: 5 minutes

 COOKING TIME: 5 minutes

Prepare this pudding just before the main course is to be served and store it in the freezer or ice compartment of the refrigerator, ready to be cooked when required.

12 oz/350 g raspberries, fresh or thawed
1 litre Wall's Italiano Choc 'n' Hazelnut ice cream
¼ pint/150 ml double cream, whipped
3 tablespoons/3 × 15 ml spoon demerara sugar

Place the raspberries in the bottom of a deep, 2 pint/1.2 litre soufflé dish. Spoon the ice cream on top and spread the cream over the surface evenly. Sprinkle it thickly with demerara sugar and put into the freezer or ice compartment.

When required, place the dish under a hot preheated grill and cook until the sugar has caramelised. Serve immediately.

Cherry Ring
Serves 6

 PREPARATION TIME: 5 minutes

 COOKING TIME: 3 minutes

35¼ fl oz/1 litre Wall's Italiano Black Cherry ice cream
6 well-baked meringue shells
For the sauce
15 oz/425 g can pitted black cherries
1 teaspoon/5 ml spoon arrowroot powder

Put the ice cream into a bowl. Break up the meringues, stir them into the ice cream and spoon the mixture into a 1¾ pint/ 1 litre ring mould. Place in the freezer for a minimum of 30 minutes.

Strain the black cherries, and mix a little of the syrup with the arrowroot in a pan to make a smooth paste. Stir in the rest of the syrup and, stirring all the time, bring the sauce to the boil to clear and thicken. Stir in the cherries and leave the sauce on one side to cool.

To serve the dessert, dip the ring mould into hot water for the quick count of 5 and invert it on a serving dish. Spoon the cherries into the centre, allowing some of the sauce to trickle over the edge of the ring. Serve immediately.

ICE CREAM SAUCES AND TOPPINGS
A selection of sauces and toppings make a very delicious and instant dessert when served with ice cream. A few ideas for using them follow in the Sundae Bests section.

Melba Sauce

 PREPARATION TIME: 5 minutes

1 lb/450 g fresh or frozen raspberries
4 oz/100 g sieved icing sugar

Sieve the raspberries through a nylon sieve and gradually stir in the icing sugar to make a smooth sauce.

Butterscotch Sauce

 PREPARATION TIME: 2 minutes

 COOKING TIME: 5 minutes

2 oz/50 g light soft brown sugar
1 tablespoon/15 ml spoon golden syrup
1 oz/25 g butter
4 tablespoons/4 × 15 ml spoon water
1 teaspoon/5 ml spoon lemon juice

Slowly heat the sugar, syrup and butter together until dissolved. Bring the sauce to the boil and cook it for 2 minutes. Add the water and lemon juice and slowly beat the sauce so that it is evenly blended. Serve warm or cold.

Tutti Frutti Sauce
Make up the Butterscotch Sauce recipe but substitute 1 tablespoon/15 ml spoon orange juice for the lemon juice. When the sauce has cooled slightly, mix in ½ oz/15 g chopped glacé cherries, ½ oz/15 g chopped angelica, ½ oz/15 g chopped sultanas and 1 dessertspoon/10 ml spoon rum or a little rum essence.

Chocolate Sauce

 PREPARATION TIME: 2 minutes

 COOKING TIME: 15 minutes

6 oz/175 g plain chocolate
½ pint/300 ml cold water
4 oz/100 g caster sugar

Break the chocolate into a pan, add a little of the water and melt it slowly over a low heat. Add the sugar and rest of the water and when the sugar has dissolved simmer the sauce for 10–15 minutes, uncovered, so that it thickens. Serve warm or cold.

Sundae Bests (see p. 82): Paradise, Chocolate Mint, Rum Punch and Twilight Sundaes

Economical Chocolate Sauce

 PREPARATION TIME: 1 minute

 COOKING TIME: 5 minutes

6 tablespoons/6 × 15 ml spoon cocoa powder
1 teaspoon/5 ml spoon coffee powder
6 tablespoons/6 × 15 ml spoon soft brown sugar
½ pint/300 ml water
2 teaspoons/2 × 5 ml spoon arrowroot

Put the cocoa, coffee, sugar and water into a pan and slowly heat the mixture, stirring occasionally so that the ingredients blend together. Mix the arrowroot with a little extra water to make a smooth paste and stir into the sauce. Bring the sauce to the boil, stirring all the time, and simmer for 2–3 minutes until thickened. Serve either warm or cold.

Dark Fudge Sauce

 PREPARATION TIME: 1 minute

 COOKING TIME: 3 minutes

1 oz/25 g plain chocolate
½ oz/15 g butter
3 tablespoons/3 × 15 ml spoon milk
4 oz/100 g light soft brown sugar
1 tablespoon/15 ml spoon golden syrup
a few drops of vanilla essence

Put the chocolate, butter and milk into a pan and melt them together over a low heat. Add the sugar and syrup and stir the sauce, still over a low heat, until all the ingredients are melted and blended together. Add a few drops of vanilla essence and bring the sauce to the boil. Boil it rapidly for 1 minute then leave to cool slightly before using.

Minty Cream Sauce

 PREPARATION TIME: 2 minutes

This is a very special sauce, ideal to serve at a dinner party.

¼ pint/150 ml single cream
1–2 tablespoons/1–2 × 15 ml spoon crême de menthe liqueur
a little green colouring (optional)

Carefully mix the liqueur into the cream and add a little green colouring, if liked, to give it a good colour.
Variation To make a more economical sauce for the family, gently melt in a bowl over a pan of simmering water 4 oz/100 g chocolate mint creams, adding a little milk as required to make the correct consistency.

Crunchy Topping

 PREPARATION TIME: 2 minutes

 COOKING TIME: 5 minutes

2 oz/50 g fresh brown breadcrumbs
1 oz/25 g caster sugar
a pinch of ground cinnamon

Mix all the ingredients together and spread them on a baking tray. Place the tray under a grill and cook, turning frequently, until the topping is brown and caramelised. Leave to cool and then sprinkle over ice cream.

Nutty Topping

 PREPARATION TIME: 2 minutes

1 oz/25 g toasted oat cereal
3 tablespoons/3 × 15 ml spoon powdered malt drink
1 tablespoon/15 ml spoon drinking chocolate
1 teaspoon/5 ml spoon instant coffee powder

Mix all the ingredients together and sprinkle over ice cream when required.

SUNDAE BESTS

Here are a few ideas for quickly made sundaes using the sauce and topping recipes already given. A selection is illustrated on p. 79.

Peach Melba
Scoops of Wall's Cornish Dairy ice cream, flanked by 2 peeled fresh or canned peach halves, topped with Melba Sauce and completed with a wafer biscuit.

Chocolate Mint Sundae
Scoops of Wall's Italiano Mint Choc Chip ice cream with meringue shells smothered in Chocolate Sauce.

Twilight Sundae
Scoops of Wall's Double Choc Chip ice cream served with Minty Cream Sauce and topped with chocolate and peppermint wafer-thin mints.

Calypso Sundae
Sliced bananas tossed in orange juice, with scoops of Wall's Jamaica Rum and Raisin ice cream on top, served with Butterscotch Sauce and sprinkled with Crunchy Topping.

Paradise Sundae
Scoops of Wall's Soft Scoop Strawberry ice cream, served with Tutti Frutti Sauce and decorated with brandy snaps.

Rum Punch Sundae
Crushed chocolate biscuit soaked in rum, topped with scoops of Wall's Italiano Rum Punch ice cream and served with Dark Fudge Sauce and Nutty Topping.

Easy Entertaining

Entertaining during the week, or even at weekends, often involves too much effort for the working wife. This seems such a pity, as to see friends over a meal is a very pleasant way of spending an evening. However, in the following menus all the hard work has been cut to a minimum. The courses have been specially planned to complement each other and to fit in well with one another during preparation and cooking. Once again, the use of labour-saving equipment has been recommended wherever possible.

A Special Occasion
Serves 6

Country Pears

Beef and Bacon Casserole
Layered Potatoes
Vegetable Medley (recipe on p. 54)

Baked Alaska (recipe on p. 74)

 MENU PREPARATION TIME: 30–45 minutes

 MENU COOKING TIMES:
Normal: 2¼ hours
Automatic cooker: 2½ hours

☛ LABOUR-SAVING EQUIPMENT: Automatic cooker

Country Pears
4 oz/113 g packet Wall's Wood Smoked Ham
8 oz/225 g cottage cheese
1 tablespoon/15 ml spoon salad cream
½ oz/15 g walnuts, chopped
½ oz/15 g dates, chopped
3 large ripe dessert pears
a few lettuce leaves for garnish
½ lemon

Cut the ham into small pieces and mix it in a bowl with the
cottage cheese, salad cream, walnuts and dates. Cut 4 slices
from the lemon and keep them on one side for garnish.

Cut the pears in half; remove the stalks and cores and then
rub the cut surfaces with the remaining piece of lemon.
Arrange a lettuce leaf on each serving plate and place a pear
half on top, cut side uppermost, cutting a sliver off the bottom
if necessary so that it stands firmly. Divide the filling between
the pears, spooning it into the cavity left after the core was
removed. Garnish each with a twist of lemon before serving.
Accompany with brown bread and butter.

Beef and Bacon Casserole
I have planned the main course so that it can all be cooked in
an automatic cooker. If, however, you wish to cook any of the

dishes separately they will take about 15 minutes less if put into a pre-heated oven.

2 lb/1 kg leg of beef
2 tablespoons/2 × 15 ml spoon plain flour seasoned with salt
    and pepper
2 oz/50 g lard or dripping
7.05 oz/200 g packet Wall's Middle Bacon Rashers
2 medium onions, peeled and sliced
¼ lb/100 g button mushrooms, trimmed
½ pint/300 ml pale ale
½ pint/300 ml beef stock

Trim the beef, cut it into 1½ in./4 cm pieces and toss in the seasoned flour. Melt half the fat in a frying pan, add half the beef and fry quickly until brown. Transfer to a large casserole, then fry the rest of the beef in the remainder of the lard. Remove the rind from the bacon and cut each rasher into four. Fry quickly in the pan, until just brown and add to the beef. Fry the onions and mushrooms and when they have absorbed all the fat pour in the beer and stock and bring the liquid to the boil. Pour the liquid into the casserole, mix all the ingredients together and then set the cooker to cook the dish at 350°F/180°C/Gas Mark 4 for 2½ hours. Place the casserole on the top shelf for the first 2 hours, with the Vegetable Medley beside it, and the layered potatoes underneath. For the final half-hour transfer the potatoes to the top shelf so that they can brown.
Freezing Casseroles are, of course, excellent after being stored in the freezer. If you wish to freeze this recipe, cook for only 2 hours; then cool, pack, label and store (for up to 3 months). Thaw overnight and reheat on top of the cooker in a large pan. It will take about 15–20 minutes to become thoroughly hot. Serve the meal with buttered noodles or pilaf rice and a selection of salads or green vegetables.

Layered Potatoes
3 lb/1½ kg potatoes, peeled and thinly sliced
salt and freshly ground black pepper
2 oz/50 g butter
½ pint/300 ml milk

Smear half the butter around the inside of a shallow ovenproof dish. Layer the potatoes in the dish, adding plenty of seasoning between each layer, and arrange the slices on the top layer to overlap neatly. Spread the rest of the butter on a piece of foil and place it over the potatoes. Cook on the shelf below the casserole for 2 hours; then remove the foil, transfer the potatoes to the top shelf and cook them for the final half-hour to brown.

Midnight Movie
Serves 4

Liver Pâté

Mustard and Lemon Glazed Bacon
A selection of salads (see recipes on pp. 61–62)
Potato Salad

Ice Cream Cassata (recipe on p. 76)

 MENU PREPARATION TIME: 30–45 minutes

 MENU COOKING TIME: 1 hour 15 minutes

Liver Pâté
Wall's make delicious pâtés, available in 5.3 oz/150 g tubs. I suggest for this menu you select the Liver Pâté, but there are two other flavours that are just as tasty – Liver and Bacon and Chicken and Liver – which perhaps you can serve another time. Purchase two tubs of pâté for this menu, divide each in half and arrange each portion on a small plate garnished with lettuce, watercress and tomato wedges. Serve with hot toast.

If, however, this particular range of Wall's pâtés is unavailable in your area either serve the Liver Pâté sold in a small sausage-shaped pack, cut into slices and arranged on lettuce, or follow this very quick and easy recipe, which uses liver sausage.

4 oz/113 g packet Wall's Liver Sausage
4 oz/100 g full fat cream cheese
2 oz/50 g butter, melted
a few drops Worcestershire sauce
a pinch of curry powder
1 tablespoon/15 ml spoon sherry
1 tablespoon/15 ml spoon milk

Midnight Movie menu

Put the liver sausage and cheese in a bowl and beat the two together with a fork until well blended. Add 1 tablespoon/ 15 ml spoon melted butter, the Worcestershire sauce, curry powder, sherry and milk and mix them all together. Divide the pâté between four small cocotte dishes and level the surface. Pour a little of the remaining butter over the top and leave to harden. Serve with toast.

Note: The pâté once made and sealed with butter will keep in the refrigerator for 3–4 days.

Mustard and Lemon Glazed Bacon
1 Wall's Bacon Joint
1 tablespoon/15 ml spoon demerara sugar
grated rind of ½ lemon
1 teaspoon/5 ml spoon dry mustard

Calculate the cooking time, following the instructions on the pack. Put the joint in the centre of a large piece of foil and place the foil in a roasting tin. Mix the sugar, lemon and mustard together and sprinkle it over the top of the joint. Seal the foil edges together and cook at 350°F/180°C/Gas Mark 4. Open the foil for the last 15 minutes of cooking to allow the bacon to brown slightly.

Leave to cool completely and then serve cut into slices, arranged on a platter and garnished with lemon and cucumber slices.

Potato Salad
1½ lb/750 g potatoes, peeled
2 teaspoons/2 × 5 ml spoon salad oil
1 teaspoon/5 ml spoon vinegar
4–6 tablespoons/4–6 × 15 ml spoon salad cream
6 spring onions, trimmed and chopped
paprika pepper

Cook the potatoes in boiling salted water for 20–25 minutes, or until tender, and drain thoroughly. Cut into cubes and toss them in the oil and vinegar. Leave on one side to cool and absorb the flavours. Finally, stir in the salad cream and spring onion and turn the salad into a bowl. Sprinkle a little paprika pepper over the top before serving.

Weekend Visitors
Serves 4

Mediterranean Bake

Cumberland Flan
Duchess Potatoes
A selection of vegetables or salads (from recipes on pp. 52–54
and 61–62)

Cherry Ring (recipe on p.77)

 MENU PREPARATION TIME: 40 minutes

 MENU COOKING TIME: 35 minutes

Mediterranean Bake
1 lb/450 g courgettes
1 tablespoon/15 ml spoon cooking oil
1 oz/25 g butter
1 large onion, peeled and thinly sliced
1 clove garlic, peeled and crushed
3 oz/85 g packet Wall's French Garlic Sausage, chopped
black pepper
3 oz/75 g Cheddar cheese, grated

Wipe, trim and thinly slice the courgettes; lay the slices on a
plate, sprinkling salt between each layer. Leave the courgettes
aside, so that some of the excess moisture is drawn out by the
salt.
    Heat the oil and butter in a large frying pan, add the onion
and fry it gently for a few minutes until starting to soften; then
mix in the garlic and cook the two ingredients together until
starting to brown. Drain the courgettes and pat them dry. Add
them to the frying pan and cook quickly until brown. Stir in
the garlic sausage, with plenty of pepper. Turn the mixture
into a 1½–2 pint/1 litre shallow ovenproof dish, scatter the
cheese over the surface and leave in a cool place until required.
It can be left overnight, as long as the surface is covered.
    Bake when required on the shelf below the flan at 375°F/
190°C/Gas Mark 5 for 30 minutes or until piping hot and
golden brown. Serve with crusty bread.

Cumberland Flan
7.05 oz/200 g packet shortcrust pastry thawed *or* 6 oz/175 g
    home-made shortcrust (6 oz/175 g plain flour, 1½ oz/40 g
    margarine, 1½ oz/40 g lard)
For the filling
1 lb/454 g packet Richmond Pork Cumberland Sausage *or*
    1 lb/454 g packet Wall's Pork Thick Sausages
2 eggs (size 3)
¼ pint/150 ml single cream or milk
4 spring onions, trimmed and chopped
7.05 oz/200 g can sweetcorn kernels, drained

Line an 8 in./20 cm flan ring with the pastry and leave it in a
cool place (overnight, if liked) to rest.

Beat the eggs and cream or milk together and add plenty of
seasoning. Mix the sweetcorn and onions together and place
them in the bottom of the flan case. Arrange the Cumberland
sausage on top in a spiral or the pork thicks as spokes of a
wheel and very carefully pour in the egg liquid. Bake the flan
on the shelf above the first course at 375°F/190°C/Gas Mark 5
for 35 minutes or until well risen and golden brown. Serve hot
with vegetables or cold with a salad.

Freezing note: The flan can be made and frozen if you wish. To
reheat, place it from frozen into the oven at 375°F/190°C/Gas
Mark 5 and cook for 20–30 minutes or until piping hot. If
required cold, leave overnight in a cool place to thaw slowly.

Duchess Potatoes
1½ lb/750 g potatoes, peeled
1 oz/25 g butter
1 egg (size 2), beaten
salt and pepper
a little grated nutmeg

Cook the potatoes in boiling, salted water for about 25 minutes
or until tender. Drain, and mash until smooth. Mix in the
butter until it melts and add a little of the beaten egg, with
seasoning and nutmeg to taste. Cool the mixture slightly and
then pipe it on to greased baking trays in large swirls. Leave to
cool completely.

Carefully brush the surface with the rest of the beaten egg;
then brown the potatoes under the flan – they will take about
20 minutes.

Freezing note: Duchess potatoes freeze very well. Pipe the potato on to greased baking trays and open freeze for 24 hours; then transfer them to a rigid container and keep for up to 3 months. To cook, brush with egg glaze whilst still frozen and then thaw and heat as in recipe.

Speedy Supper
Serves 4

Liver Sausage Mousse

Gammon Dolmas in Cider Sauce
Buttered Noodles
Salad

Peach Melba (recipe on p. 82)

 MENU PREPARATION TIME: 20 minutes

 MENU COOKING TIMES:
Normal: 20 minutes
Microwave oven: 8 minutes

☞ LABOUR-SAVING EQUIPMENT: Microwave oven and
Liquidiser

Liver Sausage Mousse
4 oz/113 g packet Wall's Liver Sausage
10½ oz/298 g can condensed consommé
2 tablespoons/2 × 15 ml spoon sherry
¼ pint/150 ml soured cream
3 tablespoons/3 × 15 ml spoon water
½ oz/15 g powdered gelatine
watercress and cucumber slices for garnish

Sieve the liver sausage and mix in the consommé to make a smooth consistency. Stir in the sherry and soured cream. Put the water in a small pan, sprinkle over the gelatine and over a low heat dissolve the grains completely. Stir this liquid into the liver sausage mixture and leave on one side, stirring occasionally until about to set. Divide the mousse between four ramekin or cocotte dishes (the mixture may make enough for six dishes, depending on their size) and leave overnight to set completely. To serve, garnish each dish with a twist of cucumber and a small sprig of watercress.

Liquidiser Put all the ingredients except the dissolved gelatine into the goblet and switch on to 'Maximum' until smooth. Add the gelatine and mix for another 2 minutes; then continue as in conventional recipe.

Freezing note: Once set, this will store covered for up to 2 weeks. Thaw slowly in the refrigerator and garnish before serving.

Gammon Dolmas in Cider Sauce
3 oz/75 g fresh breadcrumbs
½ lb/225 g cooking apples, peeled, cored and coarsely grated
1 oz/25 g sultanas
1 oz/25 g chopped walnuts
1 teaspoon/5 ml spoon dried sage
2 oz/50 g butter, melted
2 × 7.05 oz/200 g packets Wall's Half Gammon Bacon Rashers
½ pint/300 ml sweet cider
1 tablespoon/15 ml spoon demerara sugar
2 teaspoons/2 × 5 ml spoon cornflour
watercress for garnish

Mix the breadcrumbs, apple, sultanas, walnuts and sage together and bind the stuffing with almost all the melted butter. Divide it between the gammon rashers and roll each up, securing the end in place with a cocktail stick.

Brown the rolls lightly in the butter left in the pan; then pour over the cider and bring the liquid to the boil. Reduce the heat, cover the pan and poach the rolls for 15 minutes or until cooked. Transfer the rolls on a draining spoon to a serving dish, sprinkle the demerara sugar over the top and keep them warm while making the sauce.

Blend the cornflour with a little water, pour in some of the hot liquid and when it is well blended mix this into the main liquid bulk. Stirring all the time, bring the sauce to the boil and cook it for a minute before spooning it over the rolls. Garnish the dish with watercress.

Microwave oven Melt the butter in a dish for 30 seconds then make the stuffing and prepare the rolls as previously described. Return them to the dish and cook on 'Roast' for 2 minutes. Pour over the cider, cover the dish and cook for a further 5 minutes. Transfer to a serving dish, stir double the quantity of cornflour into the sauce, re-cover the dish and cook for 2 more minutes to thicken the sauce. Stir it once if necessary and complete as in recipe.

RECIPE INDEX